THE
CANADIAN LIVING
MICROWAVE
COOKBOOK

THE
CANADIAN
LIVING
MICROWAVE
COOKBOOK

By Margaret Fraser and the food writers
of Canadian Living *magazine*

A RANDOM HOUSE/MADISON PRESS BOOK

Random House of Canada
1265 Aerowood Drive
Mississauga, Ontario
Canada
L4W 1B9

Canadian Cataloguing in Publication Data

Main entry under title:

A Canadian living microwave cookbook

Includes index.
ISBN 0-394-22053-6

1. Microwave cookery. I. Fraser, Margaret.
TX832.C36 1988   641.5′882   C88-093372-0

Canadian Living is a trademark of Telemedia Publishing Inc. All trademark rights, registered or unregistered, are reserved.

**Produced by
Madison Press Books
40 Madison Avenue
Toronto, Ontario
Canada
M5R 2S1**

Printed in Italy

Contents

Introduction

Microwave cooking can be a joy. If you haven't yet discovered that, my hope is that this book will show you just how versatile and useful the microwave oven can be. For years I hesitated to use my microwave oven very often, rationalizing that meal preparation was easier the conventional way, even if it took longer. Today, I can fly in the door after work and have dinner on the table in a much shorter time — *and* tasting every bit as delicious — with the help of my microwave. I am so delighted with microwave cooking that I now have three microwave ovens — a full-size, a compact and even one at our summer cottage to keep things cooler during hot weather. No longer is my microwave oven relegated to the position of coffee-reheater and frozen-food defroster. It has become a marvelous timesaving kitchen tool, as essential as a food processor or mixer. I wouldn't give up my stove, but I'd also hate to part with my microwave oven. The more you use one, the more you realize just how many things a microwave oven can do — and do beautifully.

In preparing this cookbook, we decided to concentrate on what the microwave oven cooks best — from tender cuts of meat to all types of fish and seafood and, especially, flavorful, colorful vegetables. You'll discover timesaving recipes for traditional favorites like Old Fashioned Meat Loaf (p. 63) and Country Style Beef Stew (p. 60) along with easy but elegant new dishes like Veal Chops aux Duxelles (p. 77) or Fish with Gingered Pineapple (p. 95). Some recipes, like Fiesta Nachos (p. 41), Pita Pizzas (p. 40) and Oatmeal Chocolate Squares (p. 37), are simple enough to interest kids in the kitchen.

Ten innovative menus show you how the microwave oven can be a lifesaver for all kinds of occasions — from a quick and easy after-work meal (Dinner in the Fast Lane, p. 30) to a relaxed but stylish weekend brunch (Sunny Sunday Brunch, p. 18) to exotic, international evenings (A Taste of the Orient, p. 26, and Ranchero Supper, p. 24).

The microwave oven can also save you steps no matter what you're cooking. Throughout this book we have placed helpful hints for preparing sauces, clarifying butter, making croutons and dried bread crumbs, plus tips on softening ice cream, freshening snack foods and the dozens of other ways the microwave can be your handiest kitchen helper. You'll also find valuable cooking-time charts and a complete Microwave Know-How chapter with useful information and illustrations showing basic microwave techniques.

Microwave ovens do have limitations. So we don't suggest that you bake yeast breads or cookies, or recommend any deep fat frying in your microwave oven. Where foods need a few finishing touches to look like you expect after cooking, there are directions for coatings and browning.

You probably bought a microwave oven to make your life easier and to save you time. So we've designed this cookbook to do that, too. The recipes are clearly and compactly presented so that you'll never have to turn a page while using one of them. The large and beautiful color photographs on every spread give you great ideas for garnishing and presentation. Useful information is conveyed in sidebars right next to the recipes. We want you to be able to open this book and use it easily — no matter how rushed or busy you are. Our goal is that with increased knowledge and use of your microwave oven, you'll enjoy preparing and serving meals to your family and friends as never before.

Margaret Fraser

Microwave Know-How

What do you use your microwave oven for? If you're like most of the growing number of North Americans who consider this appliance indispensable, you're using it mainly to thaw and reheat food. But that's only the beginning of what this versatile appliance can do. If you aren't taking advantage of all your microwave oven's features, we have recipes and suggestions galore to help you discover the possibilities. And if you don't already own a microwave oven, here are tips to help you select the right model to suit your needs.

MICROWAVE OVEN SIZES

It all depends on you. Go for the full-size oven or full-featured mid-size oven if: you prepare a lot of meals for the family or entertain at home; time is important to you; you are willing to devote yourself to learning how to operate your new appliance; and you have the counter space. Prices for a full-size basic oven can be less than a mid-size model (or compact) that offers more automatic features.

But be realistic. Opt for a mid-size or compact model if: you cook for one or two only; you see the oven as a great way to reheat and thaw; you plan to use the oven as a quick practical addition to your conventional stove; you are already short of counter or under-cupboard space; and you want portability. But keep in mind that most recipes are developed for the 650- to 700-watt full-size models and you must consult your oven manual for information on adapting recipes.

The smaller ovens may have lower wattages, which may mean heating and cooking times are slightly longer depending on the cavity size of the oven. There may be other limitations to what you can do in smaller ovens, such as popping corn.

MICROWAVE OVEN EXTRAS

When shopping and comparing features of various ovens, simply ask yourself: What is this feature for? Will I ever use it?
• Variable power control gives you a range of power levels for more control and versatility in cooking.
• Electronic touch pad controls are more accurate than dials.
• A memory feature allows you to program several cooking steps into the oven ahead of time.
• A turntable, built into some models, saves opening the door to rotate the dish as food cooks, but does not always eliminate stirring or rearranging foods.
• A temperature probe, inserted into food, automatically shuts the oven off when a preset internal temperature is reached. Use the probe as a guide, but since temperatures can vary in different spots in your oven, follow recipe times and test for doneness.
• An automatic sensor cooking feature calculates microwave cooking time based on the amount of steam (humidity) released into the oven as food cooks. Some ovens have automatic cooking and defrosting features based on the weight of the foods.
• Preset, delay start and auto start are all features for programming cooking to take place at a later time.

Comparison shopping and knowledge about servicing and warranty are very important.

MICROWAVE OVEN FACTS

MICROWAVE OVEN COMPONENTS
1. Oven Cavity
2. Door
3. Magnetron
4. Wave Guide
5. Mode Stirrer
6. Power Supply
7. Power Cord

How does this oven work? There's no mystery to the cooking nor should you be afraid of microwave cooking. Microwaves, a form of radiant energy, are beamed into the oven from a magnetron tube and bounce off the walls and floor of the oven, since they cannot penetrate the metal in the cavity walls. These waves pass through microwaveable containers and into the food.

Attracted to the moisture, fat and sugar in foods (yes, even dry bread has some moisture), microwaves cause molecules to vibrate at a frantic rate. This friction produces heat, which is transferred through the food and does the cooking. Since microwaves only penetrate from 1-1/2 to 2 inches (4 cm to 5 cm) into foods, the center of the food is cooked by transfer of heat to the center from the outside. A standing time (a few minutes wait after microwaving food) allows this heat transfer to complete the cooking.

In a microwave oven, instead of setting a temperature as you do in a regular oven, you select a power level. Commonly used powers are: High, Medium-High, Medium, Medium-Low and Low. Some manufacturers use numbers (1 through 10) to represent these power levels. Since ovens vary in power levels, wattages, cavity sizes and cooking features, check the manual that came with your microwave oven to make sure you use the power levels equivalent to those used in our recipes.

Since microwaves heat only the food, the walls of the oven remain relatively cool and heat is not transferred into the kitchen. In a microwave oven, the food gets hot first, then, in turn, heats the dish. Microwaved foods cool more quickly because the food loses some of its heat to the cool air surrounding it.

MICROWAVE OVEN SAFETY

GENERAL . . .

• Plug cord into three-pronged (grounded) outlet on its own circuit.
• Keep a small bowl of water in the oven to prevent damage to the microwave if it is turned on accidentally when empty. This is especially important if children are around.
• Keep pot holders or oven mitts handy; dishes become very hot even though cooking times are short.
• When you're uncovering a dish after cooking or standing time, lift cover so that steam escapes away from you in order to avoid burns.
• Never use metal cookware, metal twist ties, metal-trimmed (gold or silver) dishes, or conventional meat or candy thermometers in the oven. Label microwaveable utensils with a laundry marker for foolproof identification.
• Teach children how to use the oven safely.
• With proper use and care there is no need for microwave oven leakage tests. If the

door has been damaged and is not closing properly, if the oven has been dropped, or if the mesh screen between the glass is torn, consult your dealer for an oven check. Keeping your oven clean will help prolong the performance of your oven.
• Use *only* those containers and coverings designated for use in a microwave. Be careful of plastics and metal. Plastic storage containers, such as those used for margarine and yogurt or those meant for storage only, are not recommended for microwave use. Not all plastic wrap can be used in the microwave; make sure you use only wrap specially designated for microwave cookery. If possible, try to avoid using recycled or dyed paper towels and napkins. Aluminum foil may be used as a shield to cover small parts of food like wing tips and bone ends of drumsticks. The foil deflects microwaves and prevents overcooking. Always place foil pieces at least 1 inch (2.5 cm) apart from each other and from the walls of the oven. ▷

BEFORE STARTING . . .

• Check your new appliance for shipping damage, especially the door and its seal.
• Follow manufacturer's instruction manual for installation, operating and safety precautions.
• Plug microwave oven into a separate circuit, properly grounded. Avoid extension cords.
• Never turn on an empty oven; microwaves can damage the cavity.

WHILE COOKING . . .

• Check dishes often; if food looks as if it is drying out or boiling over, stop cooking. Stir or rearrange the food. If foods seem to be popping and make exploding sounds, there is no danger. Simply stop the oven and check that food is properly covered and plastic wrap vented. You may need to lower the power level and cook more gently.
• Remove caps or lids from jars and bottles when warming. Avoid narrow-necked jars and bottles; pressure build-up can cause boil-overs and bottles may shatter.
• Baby food should be transferred to a microwaveable dish to heat. Stir often and watch carefully.
• Always take care to remove lids, covers or plastic wrap on top of food in the oven *away* from you, to prevent steam burns on face or fingers.
• Superheated liquids that don't appear to be boiling may suddenly erupt when removed from the oven. Let liquids sit in the oven for a few seconds before removing.
• Even though dishes appear cool, the contents may be very hot. Keep oven mitts handy.
• If a fire occurs (from overcooking, metal twist ties or paper products), leave the oven door closed; turn off and unplug the appliance. The fire will go out.

CLEANING

• Wipe up spills immediately.
• Use a cloth with warm water and mild dishwashing detergent for cleaning after each use.
• Never use steel wool or metal scouring pads for stubborn cleanup jobs. Use plastic pot scrubbers.
• Keep seal around oven door clean at all times to ensure a tight fit.
• Lingering odors? Here's a fragrant blend to deodorize your oven. In a 4-cup (1 L) measure, combine 1 cup (250 mL) water, grated rind and juice of 1 lemon, and 6 whole cloves. Microwave at High for 6 minutes or until steaming and fragrant.

MICROWAVE DISHES AND UTENSILS

Take an inventory of your cupboards. Chances are that you have more than enough microwaveable dishes. Heat-resistant glass measuring cups, pie plates, baking dishes, mixing bowls, custard cups, ceramic or glass-ceramic casseroles and saucepans, pottery, stoneware and ovenproof porcelain are fine. Plastics designed for microwave ovens are great, especially if dishwasher-safe.

Before buying a microwave, make sure it will hold the size cookware you use. Will your 13- x 9-inch lasagna pan fit into the oven, even if it has a turntable? If you choose a sub-compact oven, will you be able to reheat your dinner plates? Draw around these items including the handles and take the diagrams with you when you shop for your microwave.

For liquids like soups and sauces, use a container 2 to 3 times the volume you start with, to prevent spills and boil-overs.

Heat-resistant glass measures with lids and handles are ideal; you can measure, mix, cook and even serve or pour from the same utensil. Plastic microwaveable whisks and spoons are perfect to leave right in the cooking container for stirring during cooking time.

A browning dish has a special coating applied to its underside. When preheated empty in the microwave oven, *according to the manufacturer's directions*, this coating converts microwaves to heat. Depending on the time allowed for preheating the dish, the surface becomes hot like a skillet or grill on top of the stove. As a result, eggs may be fried gently on a lightly heated browning dish or meats can be seared and browned on a browning dish preheated to maximum times recommended. *Never preheat longer than the maximum time recommended by the manufacturer.* No damage will be done to the browning dish, but the glass shelf or tray or bottom lining of your microwave may be damaged.

Browning dishes come in various sizes and shapes; some are flat and have sides and a cover (to prevent spattering), making them skillet-like. Others are shallow dishes with a raised flat center surface, making them grill-like. Our recipes call for either a browning skillet or dish depending on what type of cooking we are doing and whether sides are necessary to contain the food and any liquids.

Instant-read thermometers can take the temperature of food whether you're using a microwave or conventional oven. Make sure your thermometer is microwaveable if leaving it in food while the oven is turned on.

TEST

Here's an easy test to check whether your dishes are microwaveable. Place the cookware in the microwave oven. Beside the cookware, but not touching, place a 1/2-cup (125 mL) microwaveable measure filled with cold water. Heat at High for 1 minute. If test dish remains cool or barely warm, it is safe for microwave cooking. If it gets warm, you can use it for warming and reheating food. But if it's hot, reserve it for gracing your dining table and do not use it for microwave cooking.

Some microwave oven models come with built-in turntables to move foods through the microwaves or a mode stirrer or rotating antenna to make rotating dishes unnecessary. However, some foods will still need to be stirred or rearranged during cooking just as they do in conventional cooking. Foods will cook just as well in the microwave without a turntable; simply rotate the dish as the recipe directs. If your oven cooks so unevenly that you must turn or rearrange foods more often than suggested, a portable turntable may be what you need and can be purchased separately.

MICROWAVE HELPERS

When you decide to add to your collection of microwaveable cookware, we suggest these as the most important "helpers":
• Covered see-through 4-cup (1 L) and 8-cup (2 L) heat-resistant glass measures make good cooking utensils for sauces and puddings.
• A microwaveable spoon and whisk are great for sauces.
• A roasting rack keeps meat from steaming in its juices and is especially popular for burgers, bacon and roasts.
• A set of muffin cups, glass custard cups, a 4-cup (1 L) and an 8-cup (2 L) ring mould and an 8-cup (2 L) Bundt pan are useful for baking.
• A micro-thermometer is indispensable for cooking meats.
• A browning dish is excellent for adding color, texture and flavor to tender cuts of meat that won't brown in the short time necessary for cooking.
• A portable turntable may be useful; if your oven does not have one built in, you can buy it separately.
• A kitchen scale is helpful for weighing ingredients in order to estimate cooking times.

COVERING FOOD

Always follow the recipe, but generally — cover. Covering food promotes faster, more even cooking and prevents spattering.

WITH PLASTIC WRAP:

Covering with plastic wrap produces a moist, steamed result. Use only plastic wraps that state "microwaveable" on the package. Be sure to *vent* plastic wraps, turning back a corner of the wrap to allow excess steam to escape during cooking. Do not pierce the plastic wrap as this may cause the wrap to split open.
• For faster, even cooking of soups, stews, casseroles, vegetables.
• To steam: cooking while retaining moisture — fish, vegetables.
• To poach: cooking in a small amount of liquid — fish, poultry.
• To reheat from frozen or refrigerated state.
• To avoid spattering, especially foods high in fat.
• During standing time: in the last stage of cooking, after removal from the microwave oven, foods finish cooking by conduction of internal heat. For dense items like roasts, turkeys, large baking potatoes and yams, food should be covered with foil for standing time. Foil will contain the maximum amount of heat in the food.

WITH LID:

• A casserole lid or microwaveable plate can be used instead of plastic wrap for the same results. Steam will escape; do not worry that lids are not vented.

WITH WAXED PAPER:

• To retain moisture without steaming.
• To prevent spattering.

WITH PAPER TOWEL:

• To absorb excess fat, moisture or steam from food as it cooks and help prevent sogginess. Wrap baked goods in paper towels for reheating; set whole vegetables like eggplant or potatoes and crumb-coated foods on paper towelling. Cook bacon on paper towel-lined plate.

WITH NO COVER:

• When using a browning dish to sear or fry, even though there will be some spattering, do not cover or foods will steam-cook.
• For crumb-coated foods like breaded chicken or fish. Steam will escape away from coating, preventing sogginess.
• Baked goods like cakes, cupcakes and muffins usually don't need covering.

MICROWAVE COOKING TIMES

A range of cooking times is built into each of our recipes. Set your timer for the lowest cooking time, then check and test food. It is easy to continue cooking for a longer period if necessary. Remember, there is still a standing time for the carry-over cooking that continues after you remove food from the microwave.

COOKING TIME IS AFFECTED BY:

• **Quantity:** the more food in the oven, the longer the cooking time.
• **Shape and Arrangement:** thin ends (roasts, fish) and bones (poultry, roasts, chops) will cook first and may require shielding. Round doughnut shapes work best (no corners). Smaller pieces of food cook faster; similar sizes cook more evenly. Place food or dishes in a circular pattern in the oven, with thicker parts of food toward the outside, to cook evenly.
• **Composition:** fat and sugar attract microwaves, sometimes causing uneven cooking. Bone conducts heat, so meat beside it may overcook; compensate by using a lower power or shielding with foil.
• **Density:** potatoes and turnips or large roasts cook at a slower rate than breads or cakes because they are more dense.
• **Temperature:** room temperature food takes less time to cook; refrigerated food takes the longest.
• **Oven Cavity Size, Wattage and Power Levels:** generally, the higher the wattage, the faster food cooks. See our note on this page regarding different brands of ovens and our recipes.

Power levels in our microwave recipes are given in words and percentages (except for High which is always 100%). Since power level terminology varies from oven to oven, check your owner's manual and use whichever word or number gives you the same percentage as in our recipes, for example:

High	**100%**
Medium-High	**70%**
Medium	**50%**
Medium-Low	**30%**
Low	**10%**

These recipes have been tested in several brands of 700-watt full-size microwave ovens. If your oven is different, cooking times may have to be adjusted slightly. If your microwave has a turntable, you may not have to rotate dishes during cooking. Pay attention to the range of cooking times and tests for doneness included in all of our recipes.

MICROWAVE TECHNIQUES

Master a few easy techniques to ensure good microwaving results.

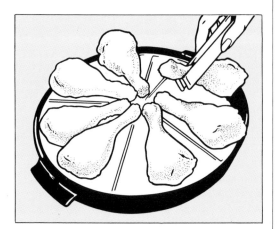

• **Arranging:** For even cooking, foods with thicker, denser portions that require longer cooking times should be arranged toward the outside edge of a dish. Try this with chicken drumsticks, asparagus spears, broccoli florets or an assortment of vegetables.

• **Rotating:** Foods that cannot be stirred, such as cake or muffin batters, layered casseroles or squashes should be rotated if necessary for even cooking. If your microwave oven is equipped with a built-in turntable, mode stirrer or rotating antenna, manual rotating may not be necessary; however, in our recipes, we include instructions to rotate as a reminder.

You can find additional microwave techniques illustrated throughout our cookbook:
• *Microwaving chicken breasts in parchment paper ovals, page 80.*
• *Starting a whole bird breast side down in a baking dish, page 84.*
• *Tenting a whole bird with aluminum foil for standing time, page 90.*
• *Folding fish fillets for uniform cooking, page 101.*
• *Arranging potatoes in a circle with thickest portions toward the outside, page 134.*
• *Shielding the corners of a square baking dish with aluminum foil, page 143.*

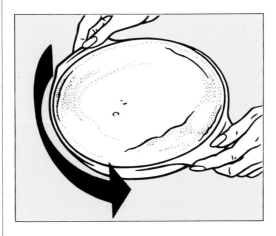

• **Covering:** Foods that benefit from steam, such as fruits, vegetables, less tender cuts of meat, and fish, should be tightly covered with a fitted lid or vented microwaveable plastic wrap. When you want excess moisture to escape, such as when cooking meat and poultry with skin, cover loosely with waxed paper, to protect oven from spattering. A paper towel (do not use any from recycled and dyed paper) is useful for covering bacon or sausages.

• **Shielding:** When cooking or defrosting large, unevenly shaped foods (whole chicken) or thin pieces of food (fish fillets), small strips of aluminum foil can be used to prevent overcooking. Place directly on wing tips, bone ends or areas that are cooking too quickly. Always place foil pieces at least 1 inch (2.5 cm) apart from each other and from the microwave oven walls.

• **Stirring:** Stir sauces, stews, soups, saucy casseroles or vegetables to ensure even cooking. Always stir from the outside edges toward the center.

CONVERTING A RECIPE

Remember the things that a microwave oven does well, such as boiling, steaming, poaching, etc. Most stove-top recipes like those for sauces, vegetables and casseroles convert easily. Start with one of these. And remember, you don't have to do it *all* in the microwave.

Don't try to convert recipes for a crowd, for cripsy items, deep-fried foods, puff pastry, angel food or chiffon cakes, yeast breads, or foods that need an even, dry heat for best results.

Look first for a similar recipe in this book or in your owner's manual/cookbook.

TIPS FOR MAKING YOUR RECIPE MICROWAVEABLE:

• Larger, microwaveable utensils (see page 10) will be necessary. Round or doughnut-shaped containers are best.

• You can probably reduce the amount of fat for sautéing or browning foods in a recipe. Since foods won't stick to pans, fat is only needed for flavor and texture.

• Reduce liquid because thickening by evaporation will not likely occur. You may need to add a thickener like cornstarch or flour.

• Reduce seasonings slightly; microwaving often intensifies or modifies flavors because of a shorter cooking time.

• Generally, salt and pepper are added at the end of cooking, always to taste. Unless there is liquid to dissolve the salt, it may cause dark spots on some foods.

• Know your own microwave oven's power levels: if a stew or pot roast needs a long, slow cooking to tenderize, or cheese and eggs need low heat to prevent curdling or toughening, cook these foods at Medium (50%) or even Medium-Low (30%).

• Decrease the cooking time, of course, and preheating is eliminated. Start with one-quarter to one-third of the conventional cooking time, then test for doneness the same way you would in the original recipe. Always allow for cooking to continue during standing time.

• Make notes; keep track of *your* own cooking times when converting recipes.

• Taste as you cook, just as you would with conventional cooking, but be careful; foods can be very hot.

• You may change the order of adding ingredients. Add cheese towards the end of cooking, just to melt and not toughen it.

• Pasta and rice are usually cooked before adding to recipes. No-boil (precooked) pasta works well. Rice may be precooked in the microwave; cook pasta conventionally on top of the stove.

• Cakes and muffins rise more in the microwave oven than in the conventional oven so never fill muffin cups or cake dishes more than half-full.

• Beating with a wooden spoon is better than a mixer for incorporating less air into cakes. You may have to reduce the leavening slightly; start with three-quarters of the amount normally called for.

TANDEM COOKING

Teamwork in the kitchen makes for perfect meals. You don't always use just your oven or frying pan to cook a complete meal. Your microwave works well with other forms of cooking, too. We call it tandem cooking — using your microwave to start the cooking, then finishing it on the barbecue or under the broiler. For example, crisp and brown microwaved scalloped potatoes or the skin on chicken under the broiler. Be sure cookware is both microwaveable and oven-proof. Take food hot from the microwave and it will finish cooking in no time under the broiler. Or start dinner preparation in the microwave oven in the morning (especially if you're dashing off to work); then finish the meal when you get home at night.

Teaming your microwave oven with your barbecue means you keep the heat out of the kitchen; enjoy foods that might dry out with a long cooking time on the barbecue; and produce a winning combination of meat or poultry that's crisp on the outside, moist and tender on the inside. The reverse is also true: barbecued foods may be frozen and reheated in the microwave for great barbecue flavor (see Microwave Reheating Guide, page 172).

TIPS AT A GLANCE FOR MASTERING THE MICROWAVE

DON'T EVEN TRY TO . . .

- boil eggs in the shell.
- melt paraffin.
- pop corn kernels in a brown paper bag.
- deep-fry.
- home-can fruit, vegetables or meat.
- bake classic soufflés, popovers, éclairs and cream puffs, angel food or chiffon cakes (in short, anything requiring dry heat to produce a crust or shell).
- bake puff pastry.
- sterilize baby bottles or preserving jars.

HOW TO SCHEDULE A MEAL

- Check recipes; start with dishes that need to be cooked and cooled.
- Continue with dishes that require standing time.
- During standing time, microwave quick-cooking vegetables, heat rolls and toss a salad.
- Nobody says you have to do it all in the microwave oven. Coordinate the meal with stove-top and conventional oven help.

The Microwave Cooking Reference Guide at the back of this book has handy charts for defrosting, cooking and reheating foods as well as many useful microwave shortcuts. If you're a beginner, start out with simple recipes, like Chicken with Herbs and Mushrooms (p. 83), Fish with Gingered Pineapple (p. 95), or Tomatoes Parmesan (p. 35). Soon you'll enjoy making more elaborate dishes, perhaps Stuffed Pork Tenderloin (p. 34) or Mediterranean Fish Stew (p. 104).

Finally, we hope you'll experiment and begin creating your own microwave specialties, as you discover more and more ways to use this unique kitchen tool.

Microwave Menus

Here are ten innovative menus that demonstrate just how helpful the microwave can be for a variety of meals and occasions – from everyday cooking for the family to stylish entertaining for a crowd. Lunch on the Terrace (p. 20), for example, makes a cool and light summer meal, while the Ranchero Supper (p. 24) is full of spicy Tex-Mex flavors. There's even a meal the kids can prepare when their friends drop by (p. 36). Remember, these menus are here to give you ideas, so feel free to add or substitute other recipes to suit your tastes.

It's easy to create your own fabulous microwave menus. Here's an example: (Clockwise from top right) Vegetable Medley (p. 124); Stuffed Pork Tenderloin (p. 34); Greens with Vinaigrette; Cheese and Cornmeal Scones (p. 138); Chocolate Mocha Pudding (p. 152)

Sunny Sunday Brunch

FOR SIX

Here's an easy menu for a relaxed Sunday brunch. Orange-flavored Sunny Eggs in a Spinach Ring make an appetizing and beautiful main dish. Serve them with Nutty Orange Bran Muffins, delectable coffee cake and cups of rich espresso.

FUZZY NAVELS or CHAMPAGNE AND ORANGE JUICE

SUNNY EGGS IN A SPINACH RING*

NUTTY ORANGE BRAN MUFFINS
(recipe, p. 137)

CRUNCHY COCOA-CINNAMON COFFEE CAKE
(recipe, p. 142)

ESPRESSO COFFEE

*Recipe appears on this page.

(Clockwise from top) Champagne and Orange Juice; Nutty Orange Bran Muffins; Sunny Eggs in a Spinach Ring; Crunchy Cocoa-Cinnamon Coffee Cake

SUNNY EGGS IN A SPINACH RING

If you don't have a ring mould, use a 10- to 12-cup (2.5 to 3 L) casserole with a greased custard cup inverted in the center.

2 cups	water	500 mL
1 tsp	vegetable oil	5 mL
1 cup	long-grain rice	250 mL
1/2 tsp	salt	2 mL
2	pkg (each 10 oz/ 284 g) spinach	2
2 tbsp	butter	25 mL
2 tbsp	all-purpose flour	25 mL
1 cup	milk	250 mL
1/4 cup	freshly grated Parmesan cheese	50 mL
1 tsp	nutmeg	5 mL
	Pepper	
3	eggs, beaten	3
2 tsp	lemon juice	25 mL
	Sunny Eggs (recipe follows)	
	Orange quarters	

• In 8-cup (2 L) casserole, combine water and oil; cover and microwave at High for 5 minutes or until boiling. Stir in rice and salt; cover and microwave at High for 9 minutes or until most of the water has been absorbed, rotating twice. Let stand for 10 minutes or until all water has been absorbed.

• Wash spinach and place in 16-cup (4 L) casserole with just the water clinging to leaves; cover and microwave at High for 8 to 9 minutes or just until wilted, rotating dish once. Let stand for 1 minute; drain. Chop spinach finely and set aside.

• In 4-cup (1 L) measure, microwave butter at High for 30 seconds; stir in flour and microwave at High for 30 to 40 seconds or until bubbly. Blend in milk; microwave at High for 3 to 4 minutes or until thickened, stirring after each minute. Stir in cheese, nutmeg, and pepper to taste; gradually stir in eggs.

• In bowl, combine lemon juice, spinach and rice. Stir in cheese sauce and mix well. Spoon into greased 7-cup (1.8 L) ring mould and microwave at High for 8 to 9 minutes or until almost set, rotating dish once. Let stand for 5 minutes. Run knife around inside of mould and unmould.

• Mound Sunny Eggs in center of ring and garnish with orange quarters. Makes about 6 servings.

SUNNY EGGS:

9	eggs	9
1/2 cup	orange juice	125 mL
1 tbsp	grated orange rind	15 mL
	Salt and pepper	

• In 8-cup (2 L) bowl, combine eggs, orange juice, rind, and salt and pepper to taste; beat until foamy. Cover with vented plastic wrap and microwave at High for 3 minutes, stirring 3 times. Reduce power to Medium (50%) and cook for 2-1/2 minutes or until eggs are creamy but not completely cooked, stirring every 20 seconds. Let stand for 2 minutes.

Lunch
on the Terrace

FOR FOUR

Summertime and the living is easy. Spinach and watercress, fresh from the garden, combine in a summery soup. A delicate scallop salad and savory scones, followed by a heavenly strawberry mousse provide a light, cool meal to serve on the patio on a warm summer evening.

SPINACH AND WATERCRESS SOUP
(recipe, p. 46)

MARINATED SCALLOP AND VEGETABLE SALAD*

CHEESE AND CORNMEAL SCONES
(recipe, p. 138)

STRAWBERRY MOUSSE*

*Recipes appear on these two pages.

(Clockwise from bottom) Cheese and Cornmeal Scones; Marinated Scallop and Vegetable Salad; Strawberry Mousse

MARINATED SCALLOP AND VEGETABLE SALAD

You can garnish this salad with shiitake mushrooms if desired.

2	pkg (each 7 oz/ 198 g) frozen scallops	2
1	medium zucchini	1
1	carrot	1
2 tbsp	water	25 mL
1-1/2 cups	sliced mushrooms	375 mL
1/4 cup	chopped chives	50 mL
	Bibb lettuce	
	Cherry tomatoes	
MARINADE:		
1 cup	vegetable oil	250 mL
1/4 cup	lemon juice	50 mL
1/4 cup	white wine vinegar	50 mL
1 tbsp	chopped fresh basil (or 1 tsp/5 mL dried)	15 mL
1/2 tsp	each granulated sugar, dry mustard and salt	2 mL
1/4 tsp	pepper	1 mL
1	clove garlic, minced	1

• Spread scallops in shallow dish. Cover with waxed paper; microwave at High for 5 minutes or until opaque, stirring once. Let stand for 5 minutes; drain and set aside.

• Cut zucchini and carrot into julienne strips; place zucchini in center of shallow dish and carrot around edge. Sprinkle with water; cover with plastic wrap. Microwave at High for 3 minutes or until tender-crisp, rotating dish once. Let stand, covered, for 2 minutes. Drain and set aside.

• **Marinade:** Stir together oil, lemon juice, vinegar, basil, sugar, mustard, salt, pepper and garlic. In plastic bag, combine scallops, mushrooms and chives. In separate bag, place zucchini and carrots. Pour 1/2 cup (125 mL) of the marinade over each. Reserve remaining marinade. Press air out; secure with twist ties. Refrigerate for at least 4 hours or overnight.

• Drain vegetables and scallop mixture; divide among 4 lettuce-lined plates. Garnish with tomatoes; pass reserved marinade separately. Makes 4 servings.

STRAWBERRY MOUSSE

In season, substitute crushed raspberries for the strawberry purée. Use the mousse as a filling for a luscious Strawberry Mousse Pie. (photo, p. 147)

1	envelope unflavored gelatin	1
1/4 cup	water	50 mL
2 tbsp	lemon juice	25 mL
1-1/4 cups	puréed strawberries (about 2-1/2 cups/ 625 mL whole strawberries)	300 mL
2	eggs, separated	2
1/2 cup	granulated sugar	125 mL
1/2 cup	whipping cream	125 mL
	Whole strawberries	

• In bowl, combine gelatin, water and lemon juice; let stand for 2 minutes or until gelatin has softened. Microwave at Medium (50%) for 1 minute. Stir in puréed strawberries. Microwave at Medium (50%) for 2 minutes; stir well. In bowl, beat egg yolks with 1/4 cup (50 mL) of the sugar; mix in strawberry-gelatin mixture. Refrigerate for about 30 minutes or until mixture begins to set.

• Beat egg whites until soft peaks form; gradually add remaining sugar, beating until stiff peaks form. Whip cream. Gently fold egg whites and whipped cream into strawberry mixture; blend well. Pour into 6-cup (1.5 L) serving dish; cover and refrigerate until set, about 2 hours. Garnish with strawberries. Makes about 6 servings.

• **To make Strawberry Mousse Pie:** Pour into prepared crumb crust (see Kiwi Lime Pie, p. 146). Refrigerate until set, about 2 hours. Garnish with sliced strawberries and sugared fresh rhubarb slices, if desired.

Romantic Dinner

FOR TWO

*For an intimate dinner with someone special, here is an elegant menu that
you can easily prepare at the end of a working day. Pop the dessert into the
microwave as you sit down to your main course. Then uncork the wine,
relax and enjoy.*

SALAD WITH WARM CHEESE NUGGETS*
LETTUCE-WRAPPED FISH BUNDLES*
BARLEY PILAF
(recipe, p. 122)
PEAR AND CRANBERRY CRISP
(recipe, p. 154)

Recipes appear on opposite page.

SALAD WITH WARM CHEESE NUGGETS

Top cool salad greens with wedges of warm goat cheese for an unusual and delicious contrast in tastes and textures.

2 oz	goat cheese	60 g
1/4 cup	olive oil	50 mL
1/4 tsp	dried basil	1 mL
1	clove garlic, minced	1
3 tbsp	whole wheat cracker crumbs	50 mL
2	green onions, sliced	2
Half	sweet red pepper, diced	Half
3 cups	torn salad greens and radicchio	750 mL
1 tbsp	white wine vinegar	15 mL
1/2 tsp	Dijon mustard	2 mL
	Salt and pepper	

• Cut cheese into 4 wedges or bite-size pieces. In bowl, combine oil, basil and garlic; add cheese, turning to coat all over. Cover and marinate at room temperature for 30 minutes.
• Dip cheese into cracker crumbs to coat; reserve oil mixture. Arrange cheese around edge of small pie plate; set aside.
• In large bowl, toss together onions, red pepper, salad greens and radicchio. Whisk together oil mixture, vinegar, mustard, and salt and pepper to taste; toss with salad greens and radicchio.
• Microwave cheese at Medium (50%) for 20 to 45 seconds or just until top of cheese feels warm to the touch. Serve salad topped with warm cheese. Makes 2 servings.

LETTUCE-WRAPPED FISH BUNDLES

If company is coming, double this recipe and take extra time to tie bundles with blanched green onion stalks before cooking. If you double the recipe, increase the cooking time by 2 to 3 minutes.

4	large romaine lettuce leaves	4
10 oz	fish fillets (orange roughy, sole, monkfish or haddock)	300 g
2	small carrots	2
1	small zucchini	1
Half	small sweet red or green pepper	Half
	Salt and pepper	
1/4 cup	dry white wine or chicken stock	50 mL
6	lemon slices	6

• Rinse lettuce leaves in cold water; shake off excess. Place on 9-inch (23 cm) pie plate and microwave at High for 20 seconds or until limp. On work surface, overlap 2 lettuce leaves slightly. Top with half of the fish, rolled up or folded over if necessary.
• Cut carrots, zucchini and red pepper into julienne strips; reserve 1/2 cup (125 mL) vegetables for garnish and place half of the remaining vegetables on top of fish. Season with salt and pepper to taste. Fold lettuce carefully around fish and vegetables, tucking in ends to form package. Transfer to pie plate, seam side down. Repeat with second fish bundle. Top with reserved vegetables.
• Pour wine over fish bundles. Cover with vented plastic wrap. Microwave at High for 2 minutes; rotate plate and microwave for 2 to 4 minutes or until fish is opaque. Garnish with lemon slices. Makes 2 servings.

(At top) Salad with Warm Cheese Nuggets; (On dinner plates) Lettuce-Wrapped Fish Bundles; Barley Pilaf

Ranchero Supper

FOR SIX

Treat family and friends to spicy dishes with Tex-Mex flavors, all made in the microwave. Precede the hearty Chile con Carne with a platter of light, crispy crudités surrounding a Mexican Cheese Dip. Round off this supper with a tequila-flavored, refreshing Margarita Pie.

MEXICAN CHEESE DIP*

VEGETABLE CRUDITÉS

CHILI CON CARNE*

MARGARITA PIE
(recipe, p. 148)

---

*Recipes appear on these two pages.

Chili con Carne; Vegetable Crudités; Mexican Cheese Dip

CHILI CON CARNE

You can dress up bowls of this chili with colorful toppings such as shredded Cheddar cheese, chopped sweet peppers, diced tomatoes, grated carrots, shredded lettuce and coarsely crushed corn chips.

1 lb	ground beef	500 g
1	clove garlic, minced	1
1	onion, chopped	1
1/2 cup	chopped celery	125 mL
1/2 cup	chopped sweet green pepper	125 mL
1	can (19 oz/540 mL) kidney beans, drained	1
1	can (19 oz/540 mL) tomatoes, drained and chopped	1
1	can (14 oz/398 mL) tomato sauce	1
1 tbsp	chili powder	15 mL
1 tbsp	brown sugar	15 mL
1/2 tsp	salt	2 mL
1/2 tsp	dried oregano	2 mL
1/4 tsp	ground cumin	1 mL

• In 12-cup (3 L) casserole, combine beef, garlic, onion, celery and green pepper; mix well to crumble beef. Microwave at High for 5 minutes or until meat is no longer pink, stirring once. Stir in kidney beans, tomatoes, tomato sauce, chili powder, sugar, salt, oregano and cumin.
• Cover with waxed paper; microwave at High for 5 minutes. Stir well and microwave at Medium-High (70%) for about 20 minutes or until desired thickness, stirring occasionally. Makes 4 to 6 servings.

Crudités go well with dips. For vibrant colors, blanch vegetables like broccoli florets, waffled carrot slices and whole green or yellow beans. Sprinkle vegetables with a little water, cover with a lid or vented plastic wrap and microwave at High for 1 minute or just until color intensifies but vegetables are still crisp. Drain and quickly refresh by plunging into cold water. Wrap in paper towels and store in plastic bags in your refrigerator until serving time.

MEXICAN CHEESE DIP

Whip up two bowls of this exotic dip—the fiery blend for your adventuresome guests and a milder version, omitting the jalapeño peppers, for the others. Serve warm with assorted vegetables or nacho chips.

1/4 lb	cream cheese	125 g
1 cup	shredded Cheddar cheese	250 mL
1/3 cup	chopped green onion	75 mL
1/4 cup	(approx) hot taco sauce	50 mL
2 tsp	chopped pickled jalapeño peppers (optional)	10 mL

• In bowl, combine cream cheese, Cheddar cheese, onion, taco sauce and jalapeño peppers (if using). Cover and microwave at Medium-High (70%) for 2 minutes or until hot and bubbly. Mix well and season with more taco sauce if desired. Serve warm. Makes about 1-1/4 cups (300 mL).

A Taste of the Orient

FOR FOUR

For a delicious dinner rich with the flavors of the Orient, try this easy menu instead of take-out. Serve delicate soup in china bowls and provide chopsticks for the vividly colored Vegetable Stir-Fry with Sesame Seeds and tangy Teriyaki Chicken. For dessert, serve Mini-Mandarin Cheesecakes and a pot of fragrant tea.

EGG DROP SOUP or ORIENTAL SOUP
(recipes, pp. 48 and 55)

TERIYAKI CHICKEN*

VEGETABLE STIR-FRY WITH SESAME SEEDS*

MINI-MANDARIN CHEESECAKES
(recipe, p. 155)

*Recipes appear on these two pages.

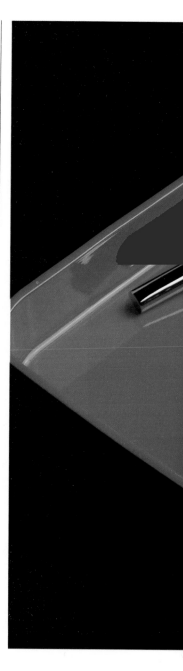

VEGETABLE STIR-FRY WITH SESAME SEEDS

This colorful stir-fry is delicious served with Teriyaki Chicken (recipe, opposite page).

2 tbsp	chicken stock	25 mL
1 tbsp	cornstarch	15 mL
2 tsp	soy sauce	10 mL
1 tbsp	vegetable oil	15 mL
3	slices gingerroot, peeled and chopped	3
1	clove garlic, minced	1
4	carrots, diagonally sliced	4
1	onion, sliced	1
Half	each sweet red and green pepper, cut in strips	Half
1/4 lb	snow peas, topped and tailed	125 g
2 cups	coarsely chopped bok choy	500 mL
	Salt and pepper	
1 tbsp	toasted sesame seeds*	15 mL

• In 1 cup (250 mL) measure, blend together stock, cornstarch and soy sauce; microwave at High for 1 to 2 minutes or until boiling, stirring once. Set aside.

• Heat microwave browning skillet at High for 5 minutes or according to manufacturer's directions. Add oil, gingerroot and garlic to skillet; stir for 30 seconds. Add carrots and onion; stir to coat with oil. Microwave at High for 1 minute.

• Add red and green peppers, snow peas, bok choy and chicken stock mixture; stir. Cover and microwave at High for 1 to 2 minutes or until vegetables are tender-crisp, stirring once. Season with salt and pepper to taste. Transfer to serving dish and sprinkle with sesame seeds. Makes about 4 servings.
*To toast seasame seeds, microwave in pie plate at High for 2 to 3 minutes or until golden, stirring twice.

Teriyaki Chicken; Vegetable Stir-Fry with Sesame Seeds

TERIYAKI CHICKEN

It's easy to keep this Teriyaki Chicken warm while you microwave the Vegetable Stir-Fry with Sesame Seeds. Simply remove the chicken to a warm serving platter and cover loosely with waxed paper and a tea towel.

1/3 cup	teriyaki sauce	75 mL
2 tbsp	packed brown sugar	25 mL
3 tbsp	vegetable oil	50 mL
2 tbsp	lemon juice	25 mL
4	boneless skinless chicken breasts (about 1 lb/500 g total)	4

• In shallow bowl or pie plate, mix together teriyaki sauce, sugar, 2 tbsp (25 mL) of the oil and lemon juice. Cut chicken into strips about 3/4 inch (2 cm) wide; add to marinade. Cover and refrigerate for 1 hour, turning occasionally.

• Heat microwave browning dish at High for 5 minutes or according to manufacturer's directions. Add remaining oil to heated dish. With slotted spoon, transfer chicken to dish and microwave at High for 2 minutes or until strips are no longer pink inside, stirring every 30 seconds. Makes about 4 servings.

Pasta Bar Buffet

FOR SIX TO EIGHT

*For a popular buffet, companion cooking makes life simple. While two
or three types of pasta cook on the stove top, you and your microwave
can make a choice of delicious sauces. Add prosciutto-wrapped breadsticks,
a tangy romaine salad and fresh fruit for dessert and
you have all the makings for a great party.*

STOVE-TOP PASTA
(Linguine, Fettucine, Rotini, or Farfalle)

BROCCOLI PESTO SAUCE
(recipe, p. 118)

CLAM AND MUSHROOM SAUCE*

EGGPLANT AND TOMATO SAUCE
(recipe, p. 123)

EASY TOMATO SAUCE*

SPAGHETTI SAUCE WITH MEAT
(recipe, p. 156)

PROSCIUTTO-WRAPPED BREADSTICKS
(sidebar, opposite page)

ROMAINE WITH PINE NUTS AND OLIVE OIL

FRESH FRUIT or MELON CHUNKS

*Recipes appear on these two pages.

EASY TOMATO SAUCE

*Delicious with meat, chicken or fish, this sauce
can double as a simple, meatless pasta sauce.*

2 tbsp	olive oil	25 mL
1	onion, finely chopped	1
2	cloves garlic, minced	2
1	can (19 oz/540 mL) tomatoes (undrained)	1
1/4 cup	tomato paste	50 mL
1/2 tsp	dried oregano	2 mL
	Salt and pepper	

• In 8-cup (2 L) measure, combine oil, onion
and garlic; microwave at High for 3 to 4
minutes or until softened.
• Add tomatoes, breaking up with wooden
spoon, tomato paste and oregano. Cover with
vented plastic wrap and microwave at High
for 5 to 7 minutes or until steaming and
slightly thickened, stirring once. Season with
salt and pepper to taste. (Sauce can be made
ahead, covered and refrigerated for up to
3 days.) Makes about 2-1/2 cups (625 mL).

*(Clockwise from top right)
Assorted Fresh Fruit;
Stove-Top Pasta; Clam
and Mushroom Sauce;
Easy Tomato Sauce;
Broccoli Pesto Sauce;
Prosciutto-Wrapped
Breadsticks*

Breadsticks wrapped in prosciutto go well with a variety of pasta dishes. Microwave 1/3 cup (75 mL) butter at Low (10%) for 20 to 40 seconds or just until softened but not melted. Blend in 1 tbsp (15 mL) nippy mustard. Spread about 1 tsp (5 mL) on each of 16 thin slices prosciutto. Wrap each slice around the center of a breadstick. Makes 16 prosciutto-wrapped breadsticks.

CLAM AND MUSHROOM SAUCE

Serve this delicious sauce over linguine or Spaghetti Squash (recipe, p. 132).

2 tbsp	butter	25 mL
1 cup	sliced mushrooms	250 mL
2 tbsp	chopped green onion	25 mL
2 tbsp	all-purpose flour	25 mL
1	can (5 oz/142 g) clams (undrained)	1
1 cup	light cream	250 mL
1/4 cup	white wine	50 mL
	Salt and pepper	

• In 4-cup (1 L) measure, microwave butter at High for 30 seconds or until melted. Stir in mushrooms and green onion; microwave at High, uncovered, for 2 to 3 minutes or until softened, stirring once. Stir in flour.

• Drain clams, reserving 1/3 cup (75 mL) juice. Gradually stir clam juice, cream and wine into mushroom mixture; microwave at High, uncovered, for 2 to 4 minutes or until mixture comes to boil and thickens, stirring once.

• Stir in clams; microwave at High for 1 minute or until heated through. Season with salt and pepper to taste. Makes about 3 cups (750 mL).

Dinner in the Fast Lane

FOR FOUR

Entertaining, even after a long day at work, can be a pleasure with the microwave. Prepare the dessert quickly in the morning before leaving for work. Later that day, prepare the meat and vegetables in minutes while the noodles cook on top of the stove. Your guests will think you've been cooking for hours.

HAM AND VEAL PATTIES WITH MUSTARD SAUCE*
BRUSSELS SPROUTS AND APPLES*
BUTTERED NOODLES
PEARS WITH ANISE
(recipe, p. 149)

*Recipes appear on these two pages.

Brussels Sprouts and Apples; Ham and Veal Patties with Mustard Sauce; Pears with Anise

HAM AND VEAL PATTIES WITH MUSTARD SAUCE

Here's a burger with a difference — ground ham in the patties. Serve with a piquant mustard sauce.

1 lb	ground veal	500 g
1/4 lb	cooked ham, ground	125 g
1	egg, beaten	1
1/2 cup	fresh bread crumbs	125 mL
2 tbsp	milk	25 mL
1/2 tsp	salt	2 mL
1/2 tsp	dried marjoram	2 mL
Pinch	ground nutmeg	Pinch
MUSTARD SAUCE:		
2 tbsp	butter	25 mL
1/2 cup	chopped onion	125 mL
3/4 cup	whipping cream	175 mL
1 tbsp	coarse-grained mustard	15 mL
2 tsp	cider vinegar	10 mL
	Salt and pepper	
GARNISH (optional):		
	Celery leaves	

• **Mustard Sauce:** In 2-cup (500 mL) measure, combine butter and onion; microwave at High for 2 to 3 minutes or until onion is tender. Stir in cream, mustard, vinegar, and salt and pepper to taste; microwave at High for 1 minute. Set aside.

• Heat 10-cup (2.5 L) browning skillet at High for 5 minutes or according to manufacturer's directions. Meanwhile, prepare patties.

• In bowl, combine veal, ham, egg, bread crumbs, milk, salt, marjoram and nutmeg; mix well and shape into 4 patties about 1 inch (2.5 cm) thick. Place patties in hot browning skillet and microwave at High for 2-1/2 minutes. Turn patties over and microwave at High for 2-1/2 minutes longer.

• Drain any fat from dish. Pour sauce over patties; microwave at Medium (50%) for 2 minutes or until heated through. Garnish with celery leaves (if using). Makes 4 servings.

BRUSSELS SPROUTS AND APPLES

Apples complement the flavor of brussels sprouts. If you prefer, you can substitute 1/2 cup (125 mL) applesauce for the apples; stir it into the casserole during the last minute of cooking.

4 cups	brussels sprouts (about 1 lb/500 g)	1 L
1/4 cup	apple juice	50 mL
2	apples, cut in 1/2-inch (1 cm) cubes	2
2 tbsp	butter, softened	25 mL
Pinch	each cinnamon and salt	Pinch

• Cut "X" in base of each sprout to permit even cooking. Place brussels sprouts in 8-cup (2 L) casserole and pour in apple juice; cover and microwave at High for 4 minutes. Add apples and microwave, covered, at High, for 4 to 5 minutes or just until apples are tender. Let stand, covered, for 2 minutes. Stir in butter, cinnamon and salt. Makes 4 servings.

Moroccan-Style Feast

FOR FOUR TO SIX

Capture the rich flavors and distinctive aromas of North African cuisine with this exotic menu. Fragrant lamb stew is accompanied by couscous and colorful, tender-crisp vegetables. Serve the salad at room temperature and offer several kinds of ripe and marinated olives. Finish with a simple fruit dessert and mint tea.

LAMB STEW WITH APRICOTS*

COUSCOUS

HERBED CARROTS WITH ONIONS
(recipe, p. 129)

RED AND GREEN PEPPER SALAD*

ASSORTED RIPE OLIVES

FLAT BREAD

SHERRIED ORANGE SLICES
(sidebar, opposite page)

MINT TEA

*Recipes appear on opposite page.

LAMB STEW WITH APRICOTS

This is a fragrant, delicately spiced lamb stew.

1/2 cup	each dried apricots and pitted prunes	125 mL
2 cups	boiling water	500 mL
1	large onion, finely chopped	1
1	clove garlic, minced	1
2 tsp	butter	10 mL
2 lb	boneless lamb shoulder, cut in 1-inch (2.5 cm) cubes	1 kg
2 tbsp	all-purpose flour	25 mL
1 cup	beef stock	250 mL
2 tbsp	tomato paste	25 mL
1 tsp	each ground coriander and cinnamon	5 mL
3/4 tsp	ground cumin	4 mL
1/2 tsp	dried mint	2 mL
	Salt and pepper	

• Place apricots and prunes in separate bowls; pour 1 cup (250 mL) boiling water over each. Let stand for 30 minutes or until plump.
• Meanwhile, in 12-cup (3 L) casserole, microwave onion, garlic and butter at High for 4 minutes or until vegetables are softened, stirring once. Toss lamb with flour; add to casserole and microwave at High, covered, for 10 minutes or until meat is browned, stirring once. Stir in stock, tomato paste, coriander, cinnamon, cumin and mint; cover and microwave at High for 5 minutes or until boiling. Stir; microwave, covered, at Medium (50%) for 25 minutes, stirring twice.
• Drain apricots and prunes; add to casserole. Microwave, covered, at Medium (50%) for 5 minutes or until meat is tender. Let stand for 10 minutes. Season with salt and pepper to taste. Makes 4 to 6 servings.

SHERRIED ORANGE SLICES
In a custard cup, mix 2 tbsp (25 mL) each sherry and brown sugar with 1/2 tsp (2 mL) cinnamon. Microwave, covered, at High for 30 to 45 seconds or until sugar is dissolved. Thinly slice 4 oranges; arrange in a low serving bowl. Pour sherry mixture over top. Cover tightly with plastic wrap; chill until serving time, at least 1 hour. Serve, garnished with shredded coconut. Makes 4 servings.

RED AND GREEN PEPPER SALAD

This colorful dish can be made several hours ahead of time and served at room temperature.

1	large green pepper, seeded	1
1	large red pepper, seeded	1
1	clove garlic, minced	1
2 tbsp	olive oil	25 mL
1 tbsp	lemon juice	15 mL
1/2 tsp	cumin	2 mL
Pinch	cinnamon	Pinch
4	green onions, sliced	4
1	large tomato, peeled, seeded and chopped	1
1 tsp	chopped fresh mint	5 mL
	Salt and pepper	

• Cut green and red peppers into chunks. In large pie plate or bowl, toss pepper chunks with garlic and oil. Microwave, covered, at High for 3 minutes, or until tender-crisp, stirring once. Add lemon juice, cumin and cinnamon; let cool to room temperature.
• At serving time, add onions, tomato and mint. Season with salt and pepper to taste. Makes 4 to 6 servings.

Simply Elegant Dinner

FOR FOUR

Start with Almond-Coated Warm Brie as an enticing appetizer. Then present a plate as beautiful as you would find in any stylish restaurant – Stuffed Pork Tenderloin complemented by Tomatoes Parmesan and whole baby carrots. Finish with a delicate Crème Caramel.

ALMOND-COATED WARM BRIE
(recipe, p. 45)

STUFFED PORK TENDERLOIN*

TOMATOES PARMESAN*

WHOLE BABY CARROTS
(chart, p. 168)

GREENS WITH VINAIGRETTE

CRÈME CARAMEL
(recipe, p. 153)

Recipes appear on these two pages.

STUFFED PORK TENDERLOIN

Buy a coarse grind of pepper, often called "coarse cracked," or crush whole peppercorns to coat these tenderloins.

2	pork tenderloins (about 10 oz/300 g each)	2
1/3 cup	tomato sauce	75 mL
1 tbsp	maple syrup	15 mL
2 tsp	soy sauce	10 mL
1 tbsp	coarse cracked pepper	15 mL
1 tbsp	vegetable oil	15 mL
1/4 cup	chicken stock	50 mL
STUFFING:		
3/4 cup	chopped broccoli	175 mL
2 tbsp	water	25 mL
3/4 cup	fresh bread crumbs	175 mL
1/3 cup	chopped walnuts	75 mL
2 tbsp	butter, melted	25 mL

• Trim fat from tenderloins. Cut each lengthwise to open flat, making extra slashes in thickest meat, but do not cut through. Set aside.

• **Stuffing:** In 2-cup (500 mL) measure, combine broccoli with water. Cover with vented plastic wrap and microwave at High for 1 minute; drain and mix with bread crumbs, walnuts and butter. Stuff each tenderloin with half of the mixture and tie tightly in several places with string.

• Combine 1 tbsp (15 mL) of the tomato sauce, maple syrup and soy sauce; spread over each stuffed tenderloin. Roll in cracked pepper.

• Heat browning skillet at High for 5 minutes or according to manufacturer's directions. Add oil, then tenderloins and microwave at High for 4 minutes. Turn and rearrange meat; cover with waxed paper and microwave at High for 4 minutes longer or until meat is no longer pink when cut in center. Remove meat from dish and let stand, covered, for 5 minutes.

• Add remaining tomato sauce to pan drippings along with chicken stock. Microwave at High for about 1-1/2 minutes or until bubbly. Strain; add any juices accumulated from meat while standing. Remove string from tenderloin. Slice and serve with sauce spooned over. Makes 4 to 6 servings.

Greens with Vinaigrette; (On dinner plate) Stuffed Pork Tenderloin; Tomato Parmesan; Whole Baby Carrots

For real Italian flavor, vary the recipe for Tomatoes Parmesan by slicing 4 tomatoes. Arrange overlapping slices in a ring on a large plate. Sprinkle with basil and pepper.

Mix together 1/4 cup (50 mL) dry bread crumbs, 1/4 cup (50 mL) grated Parmesan cheese, 1 small clove garlic, minced and 2 tbsp (25 mL) olive oil. Sprinkle over tomatoes; microwave, uncovered, at High for 3 to 5 minutes or until heated through, rotating dish twice. Makes 4 servings.

TOMATOES PARMESAN

Small firm tomatoes, lightly cooked and topped with Parmesan cheese and crumbs, are light and easy to prepare.

4	small firm tomatoes	4
1 tbsp	butter, softened	15 mL
2 tbsp	fresh bread crumbs	25 mL
2 tbsp	freshly grated Parmesan cheese	25 mL
Pinch	each dried basil and black pepper	Pinch

• Remove stems from tomatoes; invert on pie plate. With sharp knife, score an "X" on top of each tomato. Cover with vented plastic wrap and microwave at High for about 2 minutes or until tomatoes are still firm but bubbly on top.

• In small bowl, mix together butter, bread crumbs, Parmesan, basil and pepper. Spoon mixture on top of tomatoes; cover with waxed paper and microwave at High for 30 to 45 seconds or until cheese starts to melt. Makes 4 servings.

Kids'-Style Supper

FOR THREE OR FOUR

Sometimes it seems like the microwave was made just for always-hungry kids. Here are some tasty snacks they can make for themselves or their friends — to eat in front of the VCR or to serve at a party. The Ginger Honey Chicken Wings are always a big hit. And make sure they save some of the yummy Oatmeal Chocolate Squares for you.

GINGER HONEY CHICKEN WINGS*

PITA PIZZAS
(recipe, p. 40)

CRISP VEGGIE STICKS

OATMEAL CHOCOLATE SQUARES*

*Recipes appear on opposite page.

(Clockwise from top) Oatmeal Chocolate Squares; Pita Pizzas; Crisp Veggie Sticks; Ginger Honey Chicken Wings

GINGER HONEY CHICKEN WINGS

Economical, fast and easy, these subtly sweet chicken wings with Oriental flavors are perfect as tasty snacks or as a main course. Marinate them the night before or in the morning and let the kids prepare the wings as part of a quick meal.

1-1/2 lb	chicken wings	750 g
1/4 cup	honey	50 mL
2 tbsp	soy sauce	25 mL
1 tbsp	chopped gingerroot	15 mL
1 tbsp	rice vinegar	15 mL
2 tsp	lemon juice	10 mL
1 tsp	Worcestershire sauce	5 mL
1	clove garlic, minced	1
Pinch	hot pepper flakes	Pinch

• Remove and discard tips from chicken wings; separate wings at joints. Place in heavy plastic bag and set in dish.
• Combine honey, soy sauce, gingerroot, vinegar, lemon juice, Worcestershire sauce, garlic and hot pepper flakes; stir until well blended. Pour over chicken wings; press air out of bag and secure with twist tie. Marinate in refrigerator for at least 2 hours or overnight, turning bag occasionally.
• Drain wings; arrange in circle on microwave roasting rack with thickest portions toward outside. Cover with waxed paper and microwave at High for 5 to 7 minutes or until cooked, rotating dish twice and rearranging pieces if necessary.
• Transfer to baking dish and broil for 2 to 3 minutes for a browner, crispier skin. Makes about 16 appetizers, enough for 3 or 4 servings.

OATMEAL CHOCOLATE SQUARES

A crowd-pleaser if there ever was one, these bars are easy enough for young cooks to make.

3 cups	quick-cooking rolled oats	750 mL
1/2 cup	packed brown sugar	125 mL
1/4 cup	wheat germ	50 mL
1/2 cup	butter	125 mL
1/2 cup	corn syrup	125 mL
TOPPING:		
3/4 cup	semisweet chocolate chips	175 mL
1/4 cup	crunchy peanut butter	50 mL

• In large bowl, combine oats, sugar and wheat germ; cut in butter until mixture is crumbly. Stir in corn syrup. Spread mixture in ungreased 8-inch (2 L) square baking dish. Microwave at High, uncovered, for 2 minutes; stir well and press down firmly with dampened fork. Microwave at High for 1-1/2 to 2 minutes longer or until bubbly.
• **Topping:** In 2-cup (500 mL) measure, combine chocolate chips with peanut butter. Microwave at Medium-High (70%) for 1-1/2 minutes or until melted, stirring halfway through. Stir well and spread evenly over warm base. Let cool before cutting into small squares.

HOT SPICED COCOA
This makes a fast and easy after-school warm-up. In a heatproof cup or mug, mix together 1 tbsp (15 mL) unsweetened cocoa powder, 1 tbsp (15 mL) packed brown sugar, 1/4 tsp (1 mL) cinnamon; add 1 tbsp (15 mL) milk and stir to blend. In a 2-cup (500 mL) measure, microwave 1 cup (250 mL) milk, covered with vented plastic wrap, at High for 2 minutes. Pour into chocolate mixture in cup, stirring until smooth. Makes 1 serving.

Appetizers

Tasty appetizers can be turned out in minutes using the microwave. They can be as simple as crisp, raw vegetables surrounding a delicious Hot Crab Dip (p. 44) or as elegant as Almond-Coated Warm Brie (p. 45). Savory Meatballs (p. 38) and Pita Pizzas (p. 40) are perfect for half-time breaks during football season. And a dazzling array of hot and cold hors d'oeuvres – from Ginger Honey Chicken Wings (p. 37) to Beef Satays (p. 44) – make wonderful finger food for any gathering.

SAVORY MEATBALLS

Pleasantly spiced with the wonderful flavors of cumin and cinnamon, these meatballs are easy to make in a hurry. Serve with Sweet and Tangy Dipping Sauce (sidebar, p. 44) or Barbecue Sauce (see Spicy Barbecued Spareribs, p. 69).

1/2 lb	lean ground beef	250 g
1/2 lb	ground pork	250 g
1	egg, lightly beaten	1
1	small onion, finely chopped	1
1	clove garlic, minced	1
1/4 cup	dry bread crumbs	50 mL
1/4 cup	chopped fresh parsley	50 mL
1/2 tsp	salt	2 mL
1/2 tsp	pepper	2 mL
1/2 tsp	ground cumin	2 mL
1/4 tsp	cinnamon	1 mL

• In bowl, combine beef, pork, egg, onion, garlic, bread crumbs, parsley, salt, pepper, cumin and cinnamon; mix well. Shape into 1-inch (2.5 cm) balls.

• Arrange meatballs on microwave roasting rack; cover with waxed paper and microwave at High for 3 minutes. Turn meatballs over and rotate rack. Cover with waxed paper; microwave at High for 2 to 5 minutes or until no longer pink inside. Makes about 28 meatballs.

(Clockwise from top) Appetizer Frittata (p. 40); Savory Meatballs; Fiesta Nachos (p. 41); Sweet and Tangy Dipping Sauce (p. 44)

APPETIZER FRITTATA

Serve a wedge of this frittata warm, as a starter course or light luncheon dish, or reheat and serve in pita pockets. Chill it and cut diamonds and triangles to serve as finger food or snacks. Leftovers are good reheated, too. (photo, p. 39)

1 cup	packed spinach	250 mL
1 tsp	butter	5 mL
1	onion, chopped	1
1	clove garlic, chopped	1
Half	sweet red pepper, finely chopped	Half
6	eggs, lightly beaten	6
3/4 cup	fresh whole wheat bread crumbs	175 mL
1 tbsp	soy sauce	15 mL
1/4 tsp	each salt and pepper	1 mL
Dash	hot pepper sauce	Dash
1-1/2 cups	shredded orange Cheddar cheese	375 mL

• Wash spinach and shake off excess water. With just the water clinging to leaves, microwave spinach, covered with lid or vented plastic wrap, at High for 1-1/2 minutes. Drain and squeeze very dry; chop very fine and set aside.

• In bowl, microwave butter at High for about 15 seconds or until melted. Add onion and garlic; cover with vented plastic wrap and microwave at High for 2 minutes or until softened. Mix in red pepper; cover with vented plastic wrap and microwave at High for 1 minute.

• In food processor or bowl, blend together eggs, bread crumbs, soy sauce, salt, pepper and hot pepper sauce. Add cheese, spinach and onion mixture; mix well. Pour into lightly greased 9-inch (2 L) ring mould; cover with waxed paper and microwave at Medium (50%) for 3 minutes. Stir, pulling set mixture to center of mould and letting liquid run to outsides. Smooth top.

• Cover with waxed paper and microwave at Medium (50%) for 3 minutes longer; rotate dish. Microwave at Medium-Low (30%) for 10 to 12 minutes longer, rotating dish a quarter turn every 3 minutes.

• Cover tightly with plastic wrap and let stand directly on countertop for 10 minutes. If serving warm, cut into wedges. If serving cold, let cool to room temperature, then refrigerate until chilled. Makes 6 to 8 appetizer servings, or about 24 pieces.

• Freshen and crisp snack foods that have lost their crunch such as potato chips, pretzels or popcorn: Place 2 cups (500 mL) on paper towel-lined plate and microwave, uncovered, at High for 30 to 60 seconds or until warm to the touch. Let cool and serve.

• Remember, reheating appetizers right in pretty bowls, napkin-lined wicker baskets or even scallop shells makes entertaining a breeze.

PITA PIZZAS

These pizzas are quick and easy, and fun for children to make. Paper towels keep the pitas from becoming soggy as the topping heats. You can substitute 3 pitas (6 inch/15 cm round) or about 10 pitas (2 inch/5 cm round), dividing sauce and toppings evenly on rounds and adjusting cooking times.

4	pitas (about 4 inch/ 10 cm round)	4
1	can (7-1/2 oz/ 213 mL) tomato sauce	1
1/2 tsp	dried oregano	2 mL
1/2 tsp	dried basil	2 mL
1/4 lb	pepperoni, sliced	125 g
1 cup	shredded mozzarella cheese	250 mL
2 tbsp	freshly grated Parmesan cheese	25 mL

• Split pitas to make 8 rounds; arrange on large paper towel-lined plates.

• Combine tomato sauce, oregano and basil; spread about 2 tbsp (25 mL) over each round. Top with pepperoni; sprinkle with mozzarella and Parmesan cheeses.

• Microwave 3 or 4 at a time, uncovered, at Medium-High (70%) for 4 to 6 minutes or until cheese has melted and sauce is heated through, rearranging halfway through. Repeat with remaining pitas. Makes 8 pita pizzas.

Pita Pizzas

FIESTA NACHOS

For a change of pace, serve Fiesta Nachos instead of a dip in our Ranchero Supper menu (p. 24). (photo, p. 39)

1 tsp	vegetable oil	5 mL
1	clove garlic, minced	1
1	can (14 oz/398 mL) red kidney beans, drained	1
1 tsp	chili powder	5 mL
1/4 tsp	ground cumin	1 mL
Dash	hot pepper sauce	Dash
	Pepper	
36	round nacho chips (about 2-1/2 in/ 6 cm in diameter)	36
1	tomato, seeded and chopped	1
1	sweet green pepper, chopped	1
1 tbsp	finely chopped pickled jalapeño peppers (optional)	15 mL
1 cup	shredded Cheddar or Monterey Jack cheese	250 mL

• In 4-cup measure or casserole, combine oil and garlic; microwave at High for 35 to 60 seconds or until garlic is tender.

• Stir in kidney beans, chili powder, cumin and hot pepper sauce; cover with lid or vented plastic wrap and microwave at High for 2 minutes or until heated through, stirring once. Transfer to food processor or blender and process until smooth. (Alternatively, mash with fork.) Season with pepper to taste.

• Spread about 1 tsp (5 mL) bean mixture on each chip; arrange 18 chips on each of two 12-inch (30 cm) round serving dishes. Sprinkle tomato, green pepper and jalapeño pepper (if using) evenly over chips; top with cheese. Microwave one plate at a time, uncovered, at Medium (50%) for 2-1/2 to 3-1/2 minutes or until cheese melts, rearranging nachos halfway through. (Move nachos from center to outside of serving dish.) Makes 36 appetizers.

EGGPLANT DIP

Serve this dip with Pita Crisps (sidebar, this page) for a tasty and easy-to-make appetizer.

1	eggplant (1 lb/500 g)	1
1/2 tsp	salt	2 mL
2	cloves garlic, minced	2
1/3 cup	olive oil	75 mL
3 tbsp	lemon juice	50 mL

• With fork, pierce eggplant all over; wrap in paper towel and place on plate. Microwave at High for 8 to 10 minutes or until softened and skin is wrinkled, turning over halfway through. Let stand for 10 minutes or until cool enough to handle. Scoop out flesh and place in mixing bowl; stir in salt and garlic. Using electric mixer, gradually beat in oil and lemon juice. Makes about 1 cup (250 mL).

PITA CRISPS
Split 2 pita breads (about 6 inches/15 cm in diameter) to make 4 rounds. In a small bowl, microwave 1/4 cup (50 mL) butter at High for 40 to 60 seconds or until melted; brush lightly over each round. Cut each round into 8 triangles; arrange half in single layer on paper towel. Microwave

ARTICHOKE DIP

Serve this deceptively easy but delectable appetizer warm as a dip for fresh vegetables or crisp crackers.

1	can (14 oz/398 mL) artichoke hearts (packed in water)	1
1 cup	mayonnaise	250 mL
1/2 cup	freshly grated Parmesan cheese	125 mL
1/2 cup	shredded Cheddar cheese	125 mL
Pinch	paprika	Pinch
2 tbsp	toasted whole wheat cracker crumbs	25 mL

• Drain artichoke hearts. In food processor, combine artichoke hearts, mayonnaise, Parmesan and Cheddar cheeses; process for 30 seconds or until well blended. (Alternatively, chop artichoke hearts by hand and combine with mayonnaise and cheeses.)
• Transfer to microwaveable serving dish. Sprinkle with paprika. Microwave, covered with waxed paper, at Medium-High (70%) for 4 to 4-1/2 minutes or until hot, stirring after 2 minutes and after it has finished cooking. Sprinkle with crumbs. Makes 2-1/2 cups (625 mL).

WARM BEAN DIP

Just serve tortilla chips with this spicy, warm dip for a Mexican-style taste treat.

1 tbsp	vegetable oil	15 mL
1	clove garlic, minced	1
1	onion, chopped	1
1	can (19 oz/540 mL) red kidney beans, drained	1
2	tomatoes, chopped	2
1 tbsp	chopped pickled jalapeño peppers	15 mL
	Salt and pepper	
1-1/2 cups	shredded Monterey Jack cheese (6 oz/ 150 g)	375 mL
2 tbsp	chopped fresh coriander or parsley	25 mL
	Tortilla chips or sliced raw vegetables	

• In 8-cup (2 L) casserole, combine oil, garlic and onion; microwave, uncovered, at High for 2 to 3 minutes or until onions are softened, stirring once. Stir in beans, tomatoes and jalapeño peppers.
• Re-cover and microwave at High for 3 to 4 minutes or until heated through, stirring once. Mash with potato masher, leaving a few coarse pieces. Season with salt and pepper to taste. Sprinkle with cheese; microwave, uncovered, at Medium (50%) for 2 to 3 minutes or until cheese has melted. Sprinkle with coriander and serve with tortilla chips. Makes about 3-1/2 cups (875 mL).

(Clockwise from top) Artichoke Dip; Pita Crisps; Warm Bean Dip; Eggplant Dip

at High for 2-1/2 to 3 minutes or until crisp. Repeat with remaining triangles. Makes 32 crisps.

HOT CRAB DIP

The light taste of crabmeat, combined with crunchy pine nuts, makes a delicious dip with crackers or crudités.

2 tbsp	pine nuts	25 mL
1/2 lb	cream cheese	250 g
1	pkg (7 oz/200 g) frozen crabmeat, thawed or 1 can (6 oz/170 g), drained and flaked	1
2 tbsp	chopped green onion	25 mL
1 tbsp	milk	15 mL
2 tsp	lemon juice	10 mL
1 tsp	horseradish	5 mL
1/4 tsp	salt	1 mL
	Black and cayenne peppers	

• Scatter pine nuts in pie plate; microwave at High for 2 to 3 minutes or just until golden. Coarsely chop and set aside.
• In bowl, microwave cream cheese at High for 30 seconds or just until softened. Stir in crabmeat, onion, milk, lemon juice, horseradish, salt, and black and cayenne peppers to taste.
• Spoon mixture into 2-cup (500 mL) baking dish; cover with waxed paper and microwave at Medium-High (70%) for 2 to 3 minutes or until hot and bubbly, stirring every minute. Sprinkle pine nuts around outer edge of dish. Makes about 1 cup (250 mL).

BEEF SATAYS

Spicy, tender strips of beef make perfect appetizers. When cooking the satays, suspend the skewers across a ring mould so that the meat doesn't cook in the juices. A ridged roasting rack is ideal, too. Serve with Sweet and Tangy Dipping Sauce (sidebar, this page).

2	green onions, chopped	2
1	clove garlic, minced	1
2 tbsp	light soy sauce	25 mL
2 tsp	rice vinegar	10 mL
2 tsp	chopped gingerroot	10 mL
1 lb	round or flank steak	500 g
	Wooden or bamboo skewers	

• In bowl, mix together onions, garlic, soy sauce, vinegar and gingerroot.
• Slice steak across the grain into strips 1/4 inch (5 mm) thick or less; add to bowl and stir to coat. Marinate in refrigerator for at least 4 hours, stirring often.
• Thread meat onto wooden skewers, reserving marinade. Arrange skewers across ring mould; microwave, uncovered, at High for 2 minutes. Brush with marinade and rotate dish; microwave at High for 2 to 3 minutes or until meat is cooked to desired doneness. Makes about 24 appetizers.

Beef Satays

SWEET AND TANGY DIPPING SAUCE
To prepare a dipping sauce that is delicious with Savory Meatballs (recipe, p. 38) or Beef Satays, here is a simple recipe. In a small bowl, combine 1 cup (250 mL) peach jam with 2 tbsp (25 mL) finely minced crystallized or preserved ginger, 2 tbsp (25 mL) light soy sauce, 2 tbsp

ALMOND-COATED WARM BRIE

(25 mL) rice vinegar, and 1 clove garlic, minced. Cover and let stand for about 2 hours or until flavors have blended. Strain and chill if desired. Makes about 1-1/4 cups (300 mL).

Tomato slices topped with nutty warm Brie make a perfect prelude to Chicken in a Pouch with Julienne Vegetables (photo, p. 81).

1/4 cup	whole wheat cracker crumbs	50 mL
1/4 cup	finely chopped almonds	50 mL
1/2 lb	Brie cheese	125 g
2 tbsp	olive oil	25 mL
4	small tomatoes, sliced	4
1/4 cup	black olives	50 mL
1 tbsp	snipped fresh basil	15 mL

• In shallow dish, combine cracker crumbs and almonds. Slice wedge of Brie lengthwise into 1/2-inch (1 cm) thick slices, then into 2-inch (5 cm) lengths.

• Dip pieces into oil, then roll in cracker mixture, patting to make crumbs cling. Arrange in circle in 10-inch (25 cm) pie plate; cover loosely with waxed paper. Microwave at Medium (50%) for 30 to 60 seconds or until softened and heated through.

• Arrange tomato slices on individual plates; top with warm cheese. Garnish with olives and basil. Makes 4 servings.

Soups

Nothing says "comfort food" quite like homemade soup. Hearty Ham and Bean Soup (p. 49) is the perfect welcome on a wintry day. Fresh Tomato Soup (p. 52) served with crusty bread and a salad makes a great lunch or light supper. For an elegant first course, Spinach and Watercress Soup (p. 46) or smooth and creamy Parsnip and Lemon Soup (p. 52) are the perfect prelude to dinner. Best of all, now you don't have to plan ahead and then simmer for hours to enjoy rich, flavorful soups. With the microwave, you can say "soup's on!" in just half an hour or less.

SPINACH AND WATERCRESS SOUP

Brimming with garden-fresh spinach and watercress, this soup makes a perfect first course.

1 tbsp	butter	15 mL
1	leek (white part only), finely sliced	1
1	small onion, finely chopped	1
1	potato, peeled and diced	1
1/2 tsp	dried thyme	2 mL
3-1/2 cups	chicken stock	875 mL
4 cups	finely shredded spinach	1 L
1/2 cup	finely chopped watercress (about half a bunch, leaves only)	125 mL
	Salt and pepper	
	Sour cream (optional)	

• In 12-cup (3 L) casserole, combine butter, leek and onion; microwave at High for 3 to 5 minutes or until softened.
• Stir in potato, thyme and 1/2 cup (125 mL) of the stock; cover with lid or vented plastic wrap and microwave at High for 5 to 7 minutes or until potato is tender, stirring twice.
• Transfer to blender or food processor and purée. Return to dish; whisk in remaining stock.
• Add spinach and watercress; cover and microwave at High for 8 to 12 minutes or until spinach and watercress are tender and soup is heated through, stirring once. Season with salt and pepper to taste. Garnish each serving with drizzle of sour cream or blend in cream, if desired. Makes 4 servings.

(Clockwise from top) Spinach and Watercress Soup; Fresh Tomato Soup (p. 52); Winter Vegetable Soup (p. 49)

EGG DROP SOUP

To keep soup hot for about 30 minutes after preparation, cover bowl with plastic wrap and a tea towel.

4 cups	chicken stock	1 L
1/2 cup	frozen peas	125 mL
1/2 cup	finely chopped cooked chicken or pork (optional)	125 mL
1/4 cup	chopped green onions	50 mL
1 tbsp	minced gingerroot	15 mL
2 tsp	(approx) soy sauce	10 mL
1	egg, well beaten	1

• In 12-cup (3 L) casserole, combine stock, peas, chicken (if using), onions, gingerroot and soy sauce. Microwave at High for 12 to 14 minutes or until soup boils.
• In slow steady stream, drizzle egg in circular motion into soup. Season to taste with more soy sauce, if desired. Makes about 4 servings.

• To assure even cooking, meats and vegetables should be precooked before they are added to microwaved soups.
• Soups cook faster when covered. Leave headspace for soup to bubble up, but not over, and room for stirring.

HEARTY HAM AND BEAN SOUP

This hearty main-course soup is a good way to use up leftover ham.

1 tbsp	butter	15 mL
1	onion, chopped	1
1	clove garlic, minced	1
1/2 cup	diced sweet green pepper	125 mL
1/2 cup	diced celery	125 mL
2 tbsp	all-purpose flour	25 mL
2 cups	chicken stock	500 mL
1	can (28 oz/796 mL) tomatoes	1
1	can (19 oz/540 mL) romano beans	1
1 tsp	dried basil	5 mL
1 tsp	salt	5 mL
2 cups	diced cooked ham	500 mL
1/2 cup	freshly grated Parmesan cheese	125 mL

• In 12-cup (3 L) casserole or bowl, microwave butter at High for 1 minute.
• Add onion, garlic, green pepper and celery; microwave, uncovered, at High for 3 minutes or until vegetables are tender. Stir in flour and stock, blending well.
• Drain and chop tomatoes, reserving juice. Add tomatoes and beans to casserole along with their juices, basil and salt. Cover with waxed paper; microwave at High for 10 minutes. Stir in ham; microwave at High, uncovered, for 4 minutes. Sprinkle each serving with Parmesan cheese. Makes 6 to 8 servings.

Hearty Ham and Bean Soup

WINTER VEGETABLE SOUP

For a change, omit the curry powder for a milder-flavored soup. (photo, p. 47)

1 tbsp	butter	15 mL
1	onion, finely chopped	1
1	clove garlic, minced	1
1-1/2 tsp	curry powder	7 mL
1/2 tsp	ground cumin	2 mL
1/4 tsp	finely chopped gingerroot	1 mL
2-1/2 cups	chicken stock	625 mL
2 cups	julienned carrots (about 5)	500 mL
1 cup	julienned potato	250 mL
1 cup	tomato juice or vegetable cocktail	250 mL
1/2 cup	corn kernels, thawed if frozen	125 mL
	Salt and pepper	

• In 12-cup (3 L) casserole, combine butter, onion, garlic, curry powder, cumin and gingerroot; microwave, uncovered, at High for 2 to 4 minutes or until onion is tender.
• Add stock, carrots, potato and tomato juice; stir well. Cover with lid or vented plastic wrap and microwave at High for 12 to 16 minutes or until carrots and potato are tender, stirring once. Add corn; microwave, covered, at High for 2 to 4 minutes or until heated through. Season with salt and pepper to taste. Makes 4 servings.

MINESTRONE

Who doesn't love a steaming bowl of minestrone on a chilly winter day? Serve in cups as a snack or a prelude to pasta, or in large bowls with crusty Italian bread for a savory, satisfying supper.

4 cups	chicken stock	1 L
1/2 cup	small or medium shell pasta	125 mL
3	slices bacon, chopped	3
1	onion, chopped	1
1	clove garlic, minced	1
1/2 cup	chopped carrot	125 mL
1/2 cup	chopped celery	125 mL
1	can (5-1/2 oz/ 156 mL) tomato paste	1
1/2 tsp	dried basil	2 mL
Pinch	each dried thyme and hot pepper flakes	Pinch
1/2 cup	chopped zucchini	125 mL
1 cup	packed shredded spinach	250 mL
	Salt and pepper	

• In 8-cup (2 L) casserole, microwave 2 cups (500 mL) of the stock, covered with lid or vented plastic wrap, at High for 4 minutes or until boiling. Add pasta and microwave, covered, at High for 4 minutes; set aside but do not drain.
• In 12-cup (3 L) casserole, microwave bacon at High for about 3 minutes or until almost crisp, stirring twice. Stir in onion, garlic, carrot and celery; microwave, uncovered, at High for 3 to 5 minutes or until softened, stirring once.
• Mix in remaining stock, tomato paste, basil, thyme, hot pepper flakes, reserved pasta and broth; cover and microwave at High for 10 to 12 minutes or until mixture comes to boil, stirring twice.
• Add zucchini; cover and microwave at High for 3 minutes or until zucchini is tender-crisp. Stir in spinach and microwave at High, uncovered, for 1 minute. Season with salt and pepper to taste. Makes 4 to 6 servings.

CHUNKY PIZZA SOUP

The mouth-watering pizza flavors make this hearty soup a family favorite.

1/2 cup	sliced mushrooms	125 mL
1/4 cup	slivered sweet green pepper	50 mL
1	small onion, chopped	1
1	clove garlic, minced	1
1 tbsp	vegetable oil	15 mL
1	can (28 oz/796 mL) tomatoes, undrained	1
1 cup	thinly sliced pepperoni (about 5 oz/150 g)	250 mL
1/2 cup	beef stock	125 mL
1/2 tsp	dried basil	2 mL
	Salt and pepper	
1 cup	shredded mozzarella cheese	250 mL

• In 12-cup (3 L) casserole, combine mushrooms, green pepper, onion, garlic and oil; cover and microwave at High for 3 to 5 minutes or until softened, stirring once.
• Stir in tomatoes, pepperoni, beef stock and basil; cover and microwave at High for 10 to 15 minutes or until flavors are blended and soup is heated through, stirring once. Season with salt and pepper to taste.
• Ladle soup into 4 microwaveable soup bowls; sprinkle each with 1/4 cup (50 mL) of the cheese. Microwave, uncovered, at Medium (50%) for 1 to 1-1/2 minutes or until cheese melts. Serve immediately. Makes 4 servings.

Chunky Pizza Soup

Soups made ahead of time can be reheated quickly in mugs, bowls or a soup tureen. For an easy test to make sure serving dishes are microwaveable, see page 10.

ONION SOUP

This flavorful soup — with a hint of sherry — makes a terrific family supper. Team your microwave oven with the broiler for quick, delicious results.

2 tbsp	butter	25 mL
2 cups	chopped onions	500 mL
4 cups	beef stock	1 L
1/4 cup	sherry or dry white wine	50 mL
	Salt and pepper	
4	slices French bread, toasted	4
1 cup	shredded Swiss or Gruyère cheese	250 mL
2 tbsp	freshly grated Parmesan cheese	25 mL

• In 12-cup (3 L) casserole, microwave butter at High for 30 seconds or until melted. Add onions; cover with lid or vented plastic wrap and microwave for 8 minutes or until tender, stirring once.
• Add stock and microwave at High for about 5 minutes or until boiling. Stir in sherry; season with salt and pepper.
• Place four 1-1/2-cup (375 mL) ovenproof bowls on baking sheet; divide soup among bowls. Top each bowl with slice of bread; sprinkle evenly with Swiss and Parmesan cheeses. Broil for about 1 minute or until bubbly and lightly browned. Makes 4 servings.

PARSNIP AND LEMON SOUP

A pleasant combination with a refreshing taste. Instead of the pimiento swirl, hot-food fans will like 5 or 6 drops of hot pepper sauce swirled in at serving time. Spice lovers can substitute a grating of fresh nutmeg.

1 tbsp	butter	15 mL
1	large onion, finely chopped	1
2 cups	thinly sliced peeled parsnips	500 mL
1	carrot, thinly sliced	1
2 cups	chicken stock	500 mL
1 tsp	grated lemon rind	5 mL
2 tbsp	lemon juice	25 mL
1 cup	milk	250 mL
	Salt and white pepper	
4 tsp	pimiento purée*	20 mL

• In 12-cup (3 L) casserole, combine butter and onion; cover and microwave at High for 2 to 4 minutes or until softened. Stir in parsnips, carrot, stock, lemon rind and juice; cover and microwave, covered with lid or vented pastic wrap, at High for 14 to 18 minutes or until parsnips are tender, stirring once.

• Transfer to blender or food processor; purée until smooth. Return to dish and stir in milk. Cover and microwave at High for 2 to 5 minutes or until heated through, stirring once. Season with salt and pepper to taste.

• Ladle soup into serving bowls; swirl 1 tsp (5 mL) pimiento purée into each serving. Makes about 2 servings.

*In food processor or blender, process 1 jar (2 oz/57 mL) drained pimiento until smooth. Makes about 2 tbsp (30 mL).

FRESH TOMATO SOUP

Vine-ripened, juicy, fresh tomatoes make the best tomato soup. A wintry version can be made by substituting a 28 oz (796 mL) can of tomatoes, undrained, for the fresh tomatoes and adding 1 cup (250 mL) chicken stock. (photo, p. 47)

1 tbsp	olive oil	15 mL
1	small onion, finely chopped	1
1	small stalk celery, finely chopped	1
1	small carrot, finely chopped	1
1	clove garlic, minced	1
6 cups	chopped, seeded, peeled fresh tomatoes	1.5 L
1 tsp	granulated sugar	5 mL
1 tsp	dried basil	5 mL
	Salt and pepper	
	Parsley Pesto (recipe follows)	
	Herb sprigs (optional)	

• In 12-cup (3 L) dish, combine oil, onion, celery, carrot and garlic; cover and microwave at High for 5 to 7 minutes or until vegetables are tender, stirring once. Stir in tomatoes, sugar and basil; microwave at High for 5 minutes or until heated through.

• Transfer to food processor or blender and purée in batches. Return to dish; cover and microwave at High for 5 to 7 minutes or until heated through, stirring once. Season with salt and pepper to taste.

• Ladle into soup bowls; swirl 1 tbsp (15 mL) Parsley Pesto into each bowl. Garnish with fresh herb sprigs, if desired. Makes 4 servings.

VARIATION:

• To serve as a cold gazpacho version, add 1 cup (250 mL) peeled and finely chopped English cucumber and hot pepper sauce to taste after chilling.

Parsnip and Lemon Soup

For a variation on the Parsley Pesto in Fresh Tomato Soup, substitute fresh basil for half of the parsley to make a basil pesto. Or substitute fresh coriander to make a coriander (cilantro) pesto.

PARSLEY PESTO:

1 cup	tightly packed fresh parsley	250 mL
1/3 cup	freshly grated Parmesan cheese	75 mL
1/4 cup	olive oil	50 mL
1 tbsp	pine nuts	15 mL
1	clove garlic	1

• In food processor or blender, combine parsley, cheese, oil, pine nuts and garlic. Process until finely chopped. Makes 1/2 cup (125 mL).

ORIENTAL SOUP

If you can get fresh Chinese noodles, use them in place of the egg noodles.

1/4 lb	round steak, thinly sliced	125 g
1 tbsp	oyster sauce	15 mL
2 tsp	rice vinegar	10 mL
2 tsp	vegetable oil	10 mL
2	cloves garlic, minced	2
1 tbsp	finely chopped gingerroot	15 mL
2	stalks celery, diagonally sliced	2
3	green onions, sliced	3
4 cups	beef stock	1 L
1/2 tsp	pepper	2 mL
Pinch	crushed dried chilies	Pinch
1 cup	cooked medium egg noodles	250 mL
	Fresh coriander or parsley	

• In small bowl, combine steak slices, oyster sauce and vinegar; refrigerate for 1 hour. Drain, reserving any marinade.
• Heat microwave browning skillet at High for 8 minutes or according to manufacturer's directions. Pour in 1 tsp (5 mL) of the oil; add meat and toss. Microwave at High for 1 minute, stirring after 30 seconds. Transfer to bowl and set aside.
• To skillet, add remaining oil, garlic, gingerroot, celery and green onions; cover and microwave at High for 2 minutes or until slightly softened, stirring once. Stir in stock, pepper and chilies; microwave at High for 4 to 6 minutes or until heated through.
• Add noodles, beef strips and reserved marinade. Microwave at High for 2 to 3 minutes or until heated through. Serve garnished with coriander. Makes about 4 servings.

EASY FISH CHOWDER

Brimming with fish and vegetables, this hearty fish chowder is a welcome dish on a cold wintry evening.

3/4 lb	fish fillets (haddock, Boston bluefish, cod)	375 g
2 tbsp	butter	25 mL
1 cup	chopped celery	250 mL
1	onion, chopped	1
1/4 tsp	dried thyme	1 mL
3 tbsp	all-purpose flour	50 mL
1 cup	chicken stock	250 mL
1 cup	milk or light cream	250 mL
2	tomatoes, peeled, seeded and chopped	2
	Salt and pepper	
2 tbsp	chopped fresh parsley or dill	25 mL

• Cut fish into 3/4-inch (2 cm) chunks and set aside.
• In 12-cup (3 L) casserole, microwave butter at High for 30 seconds or until melted. Add celery, onion and thyme; microwave at High for 4 to 6 minutes or until softened, stirring once. Blend in flour.
• Gradually stir in stock and milk; add tomatoes. Cover with lid or vented plastic wrap and microwave at High for 8 to 10 minutes or until bubbling and thickened, stirring twice. Add fish; cover and microwave at High for 3 to 5 minutes or until heated through and fish is opaque. Season with salt and pepper to taste. Garnish with parsley. Makes 4 to 6 servings.

VARIATION:

EASY CLAM CHOWDER:

• Substitute 2 cans (5 oz/142 g each) baby clams for the fish, draining clams and reserving 1 cup (250 mL) juice to substitute for the chicken stock. After adding clams, microwave at High for 1 to 2 minutes or until heated through.

Oriental Soup

Beef, Pork, Lamb and Veal

Even though meat-and-potatoes meals are no longer routine fare for most of us, flavorful meats are just as satisfying as they always were. The microwave can give you tender, juicy meat dishes like Sweet and Sour Pork (p. 67) in a minimum of time. And sometimes using the microwave in combination with your broiler or barbecue can give you the best results of all as in our recipe for Spicy Barbecued Spareribs (p. 69). For casseroles and stews, such as Cheesy Polenta-Beef Casserole (p. 59) and Country-Style Beef Stew (p. 60), the microwave is invaluable. You can even impress company with Warm Ginger Beef Salad (p. 61) or Veal Chops Aux Duxelles (p. 77).

QUICK POT ROAST

A tender, flavorful pot roast with gravy makes a mouth-watering dinner that can be cooked easily and quickly in the microwave. Slice leftover beef thinly when cold and serve with a salad. Add a touch of horseradish or hot mustard to create hearty sandwiches.

2	onions, chopped	2
1	carrot, chopped	1
1 tbsp	granulated sugar	15 mL
1	boneless beef pot roast (3 to 4 lb/ 1.5 to 2 kg), rump, chuck or blade	1
1/2 cup	beef stock	125 mL
1/4 cup	dry red wine	50 mL
1 tbsp	tomato paste	15 mL
1 tsp	dried thyme	5 mL
1/2 tsp	whole black peppercorns	2 mL
2	cloves garlic (unpeeled)	2
1	bay leaf	1
4 tsp	cornstarch	20 mL
1 tbsp	water	15 mL
	Salt and pepper	

• In 12-cup (3 L) casserole, combine onions, carrot and sugar; microwave, uncovered, at High for 10 to 12 minutes or just until vegetables turn golden brown, stirring twice. Add pot roast; microwave at High for 2 minutes. Turn roast over; microwave at High for 2 minutes longer. Set aside.

• In 2-cup (500 mL) measure, combine stock, wine, tomato paste, thyme, peppercorns, garlic and bay leaf. Microwave at High for 1-1/2 to 2 minutes or until steaming. Pour over beef. Cover and microwave at Medium (50%) for about 1 hour or until beef is tender, turning meat over and rotating dish twice. Transfer roast to serving platter; cover and let stand for 10 minutes.

• Strain cooking liquid through sieve into 2-cup (500 mL) measure, pressing down on vegetables; skim off fat. Blend cornstarch with water; stir into cooking liquid. Microwave at High for 1 to 2 minutes or until thickened and smooth, stirring once. Season with salt and pepper to taste. Serve with pot roast. Makes 4 to 6 servings plus leftovers.

Quick Pot Roast

GENERAL TIPS

• *Always cook meats that are fresh or completely defrosted.*
• *Standing times after microwaving are essential. Roasts should be removed from the microwave 5° to 10°F (3° to 5°C) below desired temperature; internal temperature will rise during standing time.*
• *Meats cooked over 15 minutes will usually brown naturally, especially if excess fat is trimmed off. Browning agents like soy or teriyaki sauces may be brushed on meat surfaces before or during cooking to add color.*
• *To ensure a crisp brown outside coating, partially cook in the microwave; finish in the conventional oven, on the barbecue or under the broiler.*
• *Cooking time varies with type, size and shape of roast. Microwave meat*

thermometers or probes are the most accurate way to determine doneness.
• *A Medium-Low (30%) power level is considered best for tender, juicy beef and pork. Tender and medium-tender boneless cuts that are compact and uniform in shape are best for microwaving. A fresh or completely defrosted 3- to 4-lb (1.5 to 2 kg) roast, tied into a compact, even roll is ideal.*
• *Tender lamb roasts should be cooked at Medium (50%) power.*

TO COOK ROASTS IN THE MICROWAVE

• *Place roast, fat side down, on microwaveable roasting rack or on rack set in shallow baking dish.*
• *Season to taste with herbs or spices. Do not add salt (it often*

causes dark, dry spots).
• *Do not add liquid.*
• *Cover with waxed paper to prevent spattering.*
• *Turn roast over halfway through cooking and rotate dish at least once during cooking. Drain off excess fat or pan juices (these attract microwaves and alter cooking time).*
• *Shield edges that start to overcook and dry, or exposed bone ends, with smooth pieces of foil.*
• *Refer to cooking times in charts for meat being cooked and use recommended power level. Cook to desired degree of doneness before standing time, remembering that cooking continues during standing time.*
• *Let stand, tented with foil, for 10 to 20 minutes to allow internal temperature to rise and meat to "set" for ease of carving.*

BEEF ROASTS

• *To microwave tender and medium-tender roasts (rolled rib, sirloin or sirloin tip, inside or outside round, eye-of-round and rump), use Medium-Low (30%).*

Degree of Doneness	Cooking Time	Internal Temp. After Cooking	Internal Temp. After Standing Time
Rare	14 to 17 min. per lb (31 to 38 min. per kg)	130°F (55°C)	140°F (60°C)
Medium-Rare	16 to 18 min. per lb (36 to 39 min. per kg)	140°F (60°C)	150°F (65°C)
Medium	18 to 20 min. per lb (39 to 44 min. per kg)	150°F (65°C)	160°F (70°C)

PORK ROASTS

• *Bone-in roasts, like center cut loin and rib end loin, or boneless cuts, like loin (rib or tenderloin end) and shoulder butt, 3- to 3-1/2-lb (1.3 to 1.5 kg) maximum weight, are recommended for microwaving.*
• *To prevent uneven cooking of pork roasts and to ensure tender, flavorful results without concern that some*

pink spots may still exist after cooking, a covered container or a loosely sealed cooking bag is recommended. Do not pierce bag in several places, but merely tie the open end of bag loosely with string. Do not use plastic food storage bags (these are not heat-resistant and may melt). Do not use metal twist ties.
• *Roast pork at Medium-Low (30%).*

Type of Roast	Cooking Time
Bone-in	20 min. per lb (44 min. per kg)
Boneless	22 min. per lb (48 min. per kg)

• *Let stand, tented with foil, 10 minutes or until internal temperature is 170°F (80°C).*

LAMB ROASTS

• *Boneless roasts generally take about 1 to 1-1/2 minutes longer per pound (2-1/2 to 3-1/2 min per kg) than bone-in roasts.*
• *Roast lamb at Medium (50%).*

Degree of Doneness	Cooking Time For Boneless Lamb Roast	Internal Temp. After Cooking	Internal Temp. After Standing Time
Rare	9 to 14 min. per lb (20 to 31 min. per kg)	125°F (52°C)	140°F (60°C)
Medium-Rare	11 to 15 min. per lb (24 to 33 min. per kg)	135°F (57°C)	150°F (65°C)
Well-Done	13 to 16 min. per lb (29 to 36 min. per kg)	145°F (62°C)	160°F (70°C)

*Cheesy Polenta-Beef
Casserole*

**When reheating
casseroles that contain
precooked ingredients,
allow about 1-1/2
minutes per cup
(250 mL) of mixture, or
reheat to 150°F/65°C
with a temperature
probe. If you can stir the
casserole once or twice
during cooking, it can be
heated at 90% power
(reheat cycle). For
larger, unstirred
casseroles, use a lower
power (Medium to
Medium-High, 50 to
70%) and a slightly
longer cooking time.**

CHEESY POLENTA-BEEF CASSEROLE

*Preparing polenta in the microwave requires
less stirring and results in fewer lumps than
the conventional stove-top method. A mixed
green salad is the only accompaniment you'll
need for an easy family supper.*

1-3/4 cups	water	425 mL
1/2 cup	cornmeal	125 mL
2 tbsp	olive oil	25 mL
1 cup	(approx) freshly grated Parmesan cheese	250 mL
1	clove garlic, minced	1
1/3 cup	each chopped onion, carrot and celery	75 mL
3/4 lb	lean ground beef	375 g
1	can (19 oz/540 mL) tomatoes, drained and chopped	1
2 tbsp	tomato paste	25 mL
2 tsp	dried basil	10 mL
Pinch	hot pepper flakes	Pinch
	Salt and pepper	
3 tbsp	chopped fresh parsley	50 mL
	Radish sprouts (optional)	

• In 12-cup (3 L) casserole, combine water,
cornmeal and 1 tbsp (15 mL) of the oil. Cover
and microwave at High for 9 to 11 minutes
or until water is absorbed, stirring twice.
Stir in 1 cup (250 mL) Parmesan and spread
evenly in bottom of casserole; set aside.
• In 8-cup (2 L) measuring cup or casserole,
combine garlic, onion, carrot and celery.
Cover with vented plastic wrap and
microwave at High for 3 to 5 minutes or
until softened, stirring once. Stir in beef;
microwave, covered, at High for about
5 minutes or until meat is no longer pink,
breaking up meat and stirring once. Drain off
any fat.
• Stir in tomatoes, tomato paste, basil and
hot pepper flakes; microwave, covered, at
High for 10 to 15 minutes or until thickened
slightly, stirring partway through. Season
with salt and pepper to taste. Spread over
polenta and microwave, covered, at High for
4 to 5 minutes or until heated through.
Sprinkle with parsley and a little Parmesan;
garnish with radish sprouts (if using). Makes
4 servings.

Beef 59

COUNTRY-STYLE BEEF STEW

Old-fashioned beef stew is brought to new life with a touch of balsamic vinegar. We suggest you brown the meat on your stove top first for richer color.

2 lb	stewing beef, cut in 3/4-inch (2 cm) cubes	1 kg
1/3 cup	all-purpose flour	75 mL
1/4 tsp	pepper	1 mL
2 tbsp	vegetable oil	25 mL
3 cups	beef stock or hot water	750 mL
1	onion, chopped	1
1 tbsp	balsamic vinegar	15 mL
1 tbsp	tomato paste (optional)	15 mL
2 tsp	Worcestershire sauce	10 mL
1 tsp	salt	5 mL
1	clove garlic, minced	1
1	bay leaf	1
6	potatoes, cut in eighths	6
6	small whole onions	6
5	carrots, thinly sliced	5
1	stalk celery, diced	1

• Dust meat with flour and pepper. In large skillet, heat 1 tbsp (15 mL) of the oil over medium heat and brown half of the meat. Remove from skillet and repeat with remaining oil and meat. Transfer meat to 12-cup (3 L) casserole.
• Add stock to skillet and deglaze pan by stirring up brown bits. Pour over meat; stir in chopped onion, vinegar, tomato paste (if using), Worcestershire sauce, salt, garlic and bay leaf.
• Cover with microwaveable plate set right on top of mixture to keep meat immersed in liquid during cooking. Cover with lid. Microwave at High for 5 minutes; reduce to Medium (50%) and microwave, covered, for 40 minutes, stirring once during cooking. Remove plate and bay leaf.
• Stir in potatoes, small onions, carrots and celery. Microwave, covered, at Medium (70%) for 35 to 40 minutes or until meat and vegetables are tender, stirring halfway through. Let stand, covered, for 10 minutes. Makes 8 servings.

You can adapt conventional stew recipes for your microwave in the following ways:
• Cut meat and vegetables into smaller pieces than for conventional recipes.
• Rest a microwaveable plate directly on surface of the stew to keep meat immersed in liquid and prevent overcooking.
• Stir during cooking to rearrange outer and inner pieces. Foods cook faster around the outside of the dish.
• Let dish stand, covered, for 10 minutes after cooking to complete tenderizing process.

SWISS STEAK

Marinate the steak while you're at work, then pop in the microwave for less than an hour to prepare this homey dinner.

1-1/2 lb	round steak (about 1/2 inch/1 cm thick)	750 g
1	onion, chopped	1
1	clove garlic, chopped	1
1	can (7-1/2 oz/ 213 mL) tomato sauce	1
1 tbsp	vinegar	15 mL
1 tsp	packed brown sugar	5 mL
1/2 tsp	salt	2 mL
1/4 tsp	hot pepper sauce	1 mL

• Trim fat from steak; pound meat to flatten slightly and tenderize. Cut into serving-size pieces; arrange in single layer in shallow casserole.
• Combine onion, garlic, tomato sauce, vinegar, sugar, salt and pepper. Pour over steak turning pieces to coat all sides. Cover and marinate in refrigerator for at least 4 or up to 10 hours.
• Cover with lid or vented plastic wrap and microwave at Medium (50%) for 20 minutes, rotating dish twice. Turn meat over; microwave at Medium (50%) for 20 minutes longer or until tender, rotating dish twice. Let stand for 5 minutes. Makes 4 servings.

Warm Ginger Beef Salad

WARM GINGER BEEF SALAD

Ginger, crisp snow peas and soy sauce add a hint of the Orient to this quick beef salad. Serve it hot as an ideal light dinner or after-theater supper.

1 lb	boneless sirloin steak, trimmed	500 g
2 tbsp	vegetable oil	25 mL
1/2 lb	mushrooms, sliced	250 g
1/4 lb	snow peas	125 g
2 tbsp	red wine vinegar	25 mL
1 tbsp	minced fresh gingerroot	15 mL
1 tbsp	soy sauce	15 mL
1	sweet red pepper, cut in strips	1
4	green onions, sliced diagonally	4
1	clove garlic, minced	1
2 tbsp	finely chopped crystallized ginger (optional)	25 mL
4 cups	lettuce	1 L

• Slice meat into strips about 1/4 inch (5 mm) thick. Heat browning skillet at High for 6 minutes or according to manufacturer's directions. Without removing skillet from microwave oven, add 1 tbsp (15 mL) of the oil and quickly add beef; stir well. Microwave, uncovered, at High for 2 to 3 minutes or until beef is no longer pink, stirring every 30 seconds.

• Using slotted spoon, remove meat and set aside. Drain off juices, reserving 2 tbsp (25 mL). Add remaining oil to skillet along with mushrooms, peas, vinegar, gingerroot, soy sauce, red pepper, onions and garlic; stir in reserved juices.

• Cover and microwave at High for 5 to 8 minutes or until vegetables are tender-crisp, stirring twice. Return beef to skillet along with ginger (if using); let stand, covered, for 5 minutes or until heated through. Arrange on bed of lettuce. Makes about 4 servings.

SHEPHERD'S PIE

This popular old-fashioned favorite is a cinch to make in the microwave. Your family will be delighted with the tasty new additions of cheeses and sour cream to the fluffy mashed potato topping.

1-1/2 lb	potatoes (4 to 5)	750 g
2 tbsp	water	25 mL
1 lb	lean ground beef	500 g
2	eggs	2
3/4 cup	finely chopped onion	175 mL
1	clove garlic, minced	1
1 tbsp	Worcestershire sauce	15 mL
1/2 tsp	dry mustard	2 mL
1/2 tsp	(approx) salt	2 mL
1/4 tsp	(approx) pepper	1 mL
1/4 lb	cream cheese	125 g
1/2 cup	sour cream	125 mL
1 cup	shredded Cheddar cheese	250 mL

• Peel and quarter potatoes; place in shallow baking dish. Add water and cover with lid or vented plastic wrap and microwave at High for 10 to 12 minutes or until tender, stirring potatoes twice. Let stand for 5 minutes.
• Meanwhile, in large bowl, combine beef, 1 of the eggs, onion, garlic, Worcestershire sauce, mustard, salt and pepper; mix well. Press into 9-inch (23 cm) deep-dish pie plate to form shell; microwave, covered with waxed paper, at High for 3 to 5 minutes or until brown around edge and still slightly pink in center, rotating dish once. Drain and pat with paper towels to remove excess fat; set aside.
• Drain potatoes and mash. In large bowl and using electric mixer, beat cream cheese until smooth. Gradually beat in potatoes, remaining egg and sour cream. Stir in Cheddar; season with salt and pepper to taste.
• Spoon into meat shell, mounding in center; microwave at High for 6 to 8 minutes or until heated through, rotating dish twice. Makes about 4 servings.

ZESTY MEXI-BURGERS

Serve these easy burgers with all your favorite taco toppings: diced tomatoes, taco sauce, shredded lettuce, refried beans and shredded Cheddar or Monterey Jack cheese.

1	egg	1
1 lb	ground beef	500 g
1	onion, finely chopped	1
1	clove garlic, minced	1
1/4 cup	fine dry bread crumbs	50 mL
1 tsp	chili powder	5 mL
1 tsp	each ground cumin and dried oregano	5 mL
1/4 tsp	salt	1 mL
Pinch	pepper	Pinch
2 tbsp	Worcestershire sauce	25 mL
4	hamburger buns or Kaiser rolls	4

• In large bowl, whisk egg lightly. Add beef, onion, garlic, bread crumbs, chili powder, cumin, oregano, salt and pepper; mix well. Divide and shape mixture into 4 patties; arrange on roasting rack. Brush with half of the Worcestershire sauce.
• Cover patties with paper towel and microwave at High for 1-1/2 minutes; turn patties over and brush with remaining Worcestershire. Cover with paper towel and microwave at High for 2-1/2 to 3 minutes or until desired doneness, rotating rack once. Serve in buns. Makes 4 servings.

Short cooking times for meat and poultry often mean that very little browning occurs. Compensate by marinating, or brush the surfaces of hamburgers, steaks, chops, kabobs, small birds or chicken pieces with one of the following: Worcestershire, teriyaki, soy, hoisin or taco sauce, ketchup and/or mustard mixed with melted butter; marmalade, honey or tart fruit jelly.

Coating meats with whole wheat bread, cracker or cornflake crumbs, crushed potato or corn chips, tossed herbs, or shredded Cheddar or Parmesan cheese enhances their appearance.

Shepherd's Pie; Glazed
Carrots and Parsnips
(p. 128)

OLD-FASHIONED MEAT LOAF

*Meat loaf is ideal for family suppers and sliced
leftovers are wonderful for sandwiches the
next day.*

1	egg	1
1-1/2 lb	ground beef	750 g
1 cup	fresh bread crumbs	250 mL
1	onion, finely chopped	1
3/4 cup	tomato sauce	175 mL
1-1/2 tsp	salt	7 mL
1 tsp	Worcestershire sauce	5 mL
2 tsp	dry mustard	10 mL
1/4 tsp	pepper	1 mL
1 tbsp	packed brown sugar	15 mL
1 tbsp	white vinegar	15 mL

• In large bowl, beat egg until foamy. Add
beef, bread crumbs, onion, 1/2 cup (125 mL)
of the tomato sauce, salt, Worcestershire
sauce, 1 tsp (5 mL) of the mustard and
pepper; mix well.
• Form mixture into 9- x 5-inch (23 x 12 cm)
loaf; place in 11- x 7-inch (2 L) baking dish.
Cover with vented plastic wrap and
microwave at High for 5 minutes or until
meat is no longer pink, rotating dish once.
Drain off fat. Microwave, covered, at Medium
(50%) for 10 to 12 minutes or until meat is
cooked through, rotating dish twice. Drain
off fat.
• In bowl, mix together brown sugar, vinegar,
remaining tomato sauce and mustard; spread
over loaf. Microwave, uncovered, at High
for 2 minutes or until sauce is hot. Makes
about 6 servings.

CURRIED HAM STEAK

Fully cooked meats need only a short time in your microwave. Try this tasty and satisfying main course.

1 cup	orange juice	250 mL
1/4 cup	packed brown sugar	50 mL
1 tbsp	cornstarch	15 mL
1 tsp	grated orange rind	5 mL
1/2 tsp	curry powder	2 mL
Pinch	ground cloves	Pinch
1 lb	Black Forest ham steak (about 1 inch/ 2.5 cm thick)	500 g

• In 4-cup (1 L) bowl, combine orange juice, sugar, cornstarch, orange rind, curry powder and cloves. Microwave at High for 2-1/2 to 3 minutes or until mixture begins to thicken, stirring twice during last half of cooking.

• Slash outside edges of ham at 1-inch (2.5 cm) intervals to prevent meat from curling. Place in 11- x 7-inch (2 L) baking dish and pour sauce over meat. Cover with vented plastic wrap and microwave at High for 1 minute.

• Microwave at Medium (50%) for 5 to 6 minutes or until ham is heated through and flavors are blended, rotating dish and spooning sauce over ham halfway through cooking time. Let stand for 5 minutes. Makes 4 servings.

HAM AND LEEK GRATIN

Supper's all wrapped up when you serve this main dish with a spinach salad and Blackened Banana Boats (recipe, p. 149) for dessert.

8	leeks (about 3 lb/ 1.5 g total), trimmed and cleaned	8
1/4 cup	water	50 mL
4 tsp	butter	20 mL
4 tsp	all-purpose flour	20 mL
1 cup	milk	250 mL
1 cup	shredded Swiss cheese	250 mL
2 oz	cream cheese, cut in 1-inch (2.5 cm) cubes	50 g
Pinch	nutmeg	Pinch
	Salt and pepper	
8	slices Black Forest ham (about 1/2 lb/ 250 g)	8
2 tbsp	fine dry bread crumbs	25 mL

• On large round platter, arrange leeks in circle, white ends toward outside; pour water over. Cover with vented plastic wrap and microwave at High for 14 to 16 minutes or until tender, turning leeks over and rearranging halfway through. Drain off water and set leeks aside.

• In 4-cup (1 L) measuring cup, microwave butter at High for 30 to 40 seconds or until melted; stir in flour until smooth. Whisk in milk; microwave at High for 2 to 4 minutes or until sauce boils and thickens, whisking twice. Stir in Swiss and cream cheeses. Add nutmeg; season with salt and pepper to taste and set aside.

• Wrap 1 slice ham around each leek; arrange in greased 11- x 7-inch (2 L) baking dish. Pour sauce over; sprinkle with bread crumbs. Microwave at High for 6 to 8 minutes or until bubbly, rotating dish once. Makes 4 servings.

Ham and Leek Gratin

SPICY SAUSAGE PATTIES

For a hearty breakfast or brunch, serve these crisp, spicy patties accompanied by Poached Eggs with Salsa Mexicana (recipe, p. 107).

1	egg	1
1 lb	ground pork	500 g
1/2 cup	fresh bread crumbs	125 mL
1	small onion, finely chopped	1
1	clove garlic, minced	1
1-1/2 tsp	chili powder	7 mL
1/2 tsp	hot pepper sauce	2 mL
1/2 tsp	each salt, pepper and dried oregano	2 mL
1/4 tsp	each cinnamon, ground cumin and cloves	1 mL

• In large bowl, beat egg until foamy. Add pork, bread crumbs, onion, garlic, chili powder, hot pepper sauce, salt, pepper, oregano, cinnamon, cumin and cloves; mix well.

• Divide mixture into 8 equal portions and form into patties. Place on roasting rack; cover with paper towel and microwave at High for 2 minutes. Turn patties over. Microwave, covered with paper towel, at High for 3 minutes or until cooked through, rotating rack once. Makes 4 servings.

ENGLISH MIXED GRILL

Brush skewers of meat with lemon herb butter to keep them tender and juicy. Serve with Tomatoes Parmesan (recipe, p. 35) for color.

1/3 lb	English or country-style sausages	175 g
6	slices bacon	6
1/2 lb	boneless chicken breasts	250 g
1/3 lb	chicken livers	175 g
1 tbsp	lemon juice	15 mL
1 tbsp	butter, melted	15 mL
1 tsp	dried sage, thyme or rosemary	5 mL

• Arrange sausages on rack; prick with fork. Cover with paper towel and microwave at High for 1 minute. Turn sausages over and microwave at High for 2 to 3 minutes or until cooked through. Cut into 6 pieces and set aside.
• Arrange bacon on rack; cover with paper towel and microwave at High for 3 minutes. Cut in half and set aside.
• Cut chicken breasts into 12 pieces. Trim and pierce chicken livers; cut into 12 pieces. Wrap each piece of liver with bacon; thread onto 6 greased wooden skewers along with chicken and sausages. Lay skewers across 11- x 7-inch (2 L) dish to rest on edges of dish.
• Combine lemon juice, butter and sage; brush some of the mixture over kabobs, especially the livers. Microwave at High for 6 to 9 minutes or until livers are cooked and chicken is no longer pink inside, turning, rearranging and brushing kabobs every 2 minutes. Makes 4 to 6 servings.

BREADED HERB PORK CHOPS

If you don't have a browning dish, coat meats with an herbed crumb mixture — looks great and adds flavor.

1	egg	1
2 tbsp	milk	25 mL
3/4 cup	finely crushed whole wheat cracker crumbs	175 mL
1	clove garlic, minced	1
2 tbsp	chopped fresh parsley	25 mL
1/4 tsp	dried tarragon	1 mL
1/4 tsp	pepper	1 mL
4	pork chops (6 oz/ 175 g each), trimmed	4

• In shallow bowl, whisk egg with milk. In separate shallow bowl, combine cracker crumbs, garlic, parsley, tarragon and pepper.
• Dip pork chops into egg mixture, then cracker crumb mixture to coat. Place on roasting rack with meatiest portions to outside.
• Cover with paper towel and microwave at High for 8 to 10 minutes or until meat next to bone is no longer pink, rotating halfway through. Let stand, covered, for 5 minutes. Makes 4 servings.

Breaded Herb Pork Chops; Acorn Squash Ring stuffed with Cranberries and Apples (p. 126)

Sweet and Sour Pork

SWEET AND SOUR PORK

A tangy sweet-and-sour sauce combines with pork for a quick and easy main dish. Accompany with green beans and fluffy rice.

3 tbsp	soy sauce	50 mL
3 tbsp	white vinegar	50 mL
1-1/2 lb	boneless pork (butt, shoulder or leg), trimmed and cut in 3/4-inch (2 cm) cubes	750 g
1 tbsp	vegetable oil	15 mL
3	carrots, sliced	3
1	onion, chopped	1
1	sweet green pepper, chopped	1
1 cup	chicken stock	250 mL
3 tbsp	packed brown sugar	50 mL
1	can (14 oz/398 mL) pineapple chunks	1
3 tbsp	cornstarch	50 mL
	Salt and pepper	

• In bowl, combine soy sauce and vinegar; add pork cubes and stir to coat. Cover and marinate in refrigerator for 2 to 3 hours.
• In 12-cup (3 L) casserole, combine oil, carrots and onion; cover and microwave at High for 3 to 4 minutes or until softened, stirring once. Stir in green pepper, chicken stock, sugar and pork mixture.
• Drain pineapple; set chunks aside and reserve juice. Stir 1/2 cup (125 mL) of the pineapple juice into pork mixture; cover and microwave at High for 5 minutes. Microwave at Medium (50%) for 17 to 22 minutes or until pork is tender, stirring occasionally.
• Mix cornstarch with 3 tbsp (50 mL) reserved pineapple juice until smooth. Add to pork mixture along with pineapple chunks; microwave at High, uncovered, for 5 to 7 minutes or until heated through and thickened, stirring once. Season with salt and pepper to taste. Makes about 6 servings.

BRAISED HAM WITH QUICK MADEIRA SAUCE

Team this dish with Carrot Coins with Spinach (recipe, p. 128), whole wheat rolls and Blueberry-Peach Clafouti (recipe, p. 150) for a complete microwave meal.

1	pkg (10 g) dried porcini mushrooms	1
1 cup	beef stock	250 mL
1 tbsp	tomato paste	15 mL
1/2 tsp	dried thyme	2 mL
1 lb	boneless ham, smoked pork loin or Canadian back bacon	500 g
2 tbsp	cornstarch	25 mL
1/4 cup	madeira or dry sherry	50 mL

• In small bowl, soak mushrooms in 1/2 cup (125 mL) warm water for 20 to 30 minutes or until softened. Strain through paper towel- or filter paper-lined sieve into 2-cup (500 mL) measure, reserving liquid. Chop mushrooms and set aside.

• In separate 2-cup (500 mL) measure, stir together stock, tomato paste and thyme; microwave at High for 1 minute or until hot.

• Place ham on 9-inch (23 cm) pie plate; pour hot stock mixture over. Cover with vented plastic wrap and microwave at Medium (50%) for 6 to 8 minutes or until ham is heated through, rotating plate halfway through. Transfer ham to carving board, reserving juices; cover ham and keep warm.

• Dissolve cornstarch in reserved mushroom liquid; add juices from ham. Microwave at High for about 2 minutes or until thickened, stirring once. Stir mushrooms into sauce along with madeira.

• Slice ham and arrange on serving plates; spoon sauce over. Makes about 4 servings.

If dried porcini mushrooms are not available, substitute fresh button, brown or wild mushrooms. In a 4-cup (1 L) measure, toss 2 cups (500 mL) sliced mushrooms with 1 tbsp (15 mL) butter. Cover with lid or vented plastic wrap; microwave at High for 2 to 4 minutes or until tender. Use in place of dried porcini mushrooms in the Quick Madeira Sauce (this page).

LEMON-THYME PORK CHOPS

Small quantities of meat brown nicely in the microwave when you use a browning dish or skillet.

2	pork chops (about 3/4 lb/375 g total)	2
1 tbsp	olive oil	15 mL
1 tbsp	lemon juice	15 mL
2 tsp	honey	10 mL
1 tsp	Dijon mustard	5 mL
1/2 tsp	dried thyme	2 mL
1 tsp	vegetable oil	5 mL
	Salt and pepper	

• Trim fat from chops; place in shallow glass bowl. Whisk together olive oil, lemon juice, honey, mustard and thyme; pour over chops. Cover and let stand for 20 minutes at room temperature or refrigerate for up to 8 hours, turning several times.

• Heat browning dish according to manufacturer's directions. Leaving dish in oven, pour on vegetable oil and tilt dish to coat surface evenly. Place chops on dish; microwave at High for 2 minutes. Turn chops; microwave at High for 2 to 4 minutes longer or until chops are no longer pink inside. Season with salt and pepper to taste. Makes 2 servings.

SPICY BARBECUED SPARERIBS

Use the microwave oven to precook these ribs. Halfway through cooking, rearrange ribs, exposing the least-cooked parts and overlapping or covering the most-cooked pieces. Finish the ribs on the barbecue.

3 lb	pork spareribs	1.5 kg
1/4 cup	water	50 mL
BARBECUE SAUCE:		
2 tbsp	butter	25 mL
1	medium onion, chopped	1
1	clove garlic, chopped	1
1 cup	ketchup	250 mL
2 tbsp	Worcestershire sauce	25 mL
1 tbsp	vinegar	15 mL
1 tsp	dry mustard	5 mL
1 tsp	granulated sugar	5 mL
1/2 tsp	salt	2 mL
1/4 tsp	hot pepper sauce	1 mL

• **Barbecue Sauce:** In 4-cup (1 L) measure, microwave butter, onion and garlic at High for 1-1/2 to 2 minutes or until soft. Add ketchup, Worcestershire sauce, vinegar, mustard, sugar, salt and hot pepper sauce, stirring well. Microwave, uncovered, at High for 3 to 4 minutes until mixture boils, stirring several times. Makes about 1-1/2 cups (375 mL) sauce.

• Cut spareribs into serving-size pieces. Place in 12-cup (3 L) microwaveable casserole, overlapping thin pieces slightly. Add water and cover with lid or vented plastic wrap. Microwave at High for 5 minutes. Then continue to microwave, covered, at Medium (50%) for 15 to 20 minutes or until no longer pink inside, turning ribs halfway through. Drain.

• Place ribs meat side down on grill, about 4 inches (10 cm) from medium-hot coals. Brush with barbecue sauce. Grill ribs for 15 to 20 minutes or until fork-tender and browned, turning and basting with sauce every 5 minutes. Makes 4 servings.

Braised Ham with Quick Madeira Sauce; Carrot Coins with Spinach (p. 128); Blueberry-Peach Clafouti (p. 150)

CHOUCROUTE GARNIE

Choucroute Garnie

This is classic old-country-style cooking at its heartiest and robust best. Serve with Braised Potatoes (recipe, p. 133).

1	can (28 oz/798 mL) sauerkraut	1
1	onion, sliced	1
1	apple, cored and sliced	1
1/2 cup	apple juice	125 mL
2 tsp	juniper berries	10 mL
1	bay leaf	1
1/2 lb	farmer's or bratwurst sausage	250 g
1/2 lb	pork tenderloin	250 g
2	slices bacon, halved	2

• Drain and rinse sauerkraut under cold running water; drain and place in 12-cup (3 L) baking dish. Stir in onion, apple, apple juice, juniper berries and bay leaf. Prick sausage and arrange over sauerkraut along with pork and bacon. Cover with lid or vented plastic wrap and microwave at High for 10 minutes.
• Stir mixture and turn meats over. Microwave at Medium (50%) for 10 minutes or until pork is no longer pink and sausage is cooked through. Remove bay leaf. Mound sauerkraut on plates; slice meats and arrange over top along with bacon. Makes 4 servings.

Marinated Lamb Loins

MARINATED LAMB LOINS

For tender, flavorful lamb, marinate in this delicious mixture for an hour.

1/4 cup	chopped green onions	50 mL
1/4 cup	soy sauce	50 mL
1/4 cup	dry sherry	50 mL
1/4 cup	liquid honey	50 mL
1 tbsp	rice vinegar	15 mL
1	clove garlic, minced	1
1/2 tsp	ground ginger	2 mL
1/2 tsp	Chinese five-spice powder	2 mL
1-1/4 lb	lamb loins	625 g

• In large bowl, combine onions, soy sauce, sherry, honey, vinegar, garlic, ginger and five-spice powder; add lamb. Cover and marinate at room temperature for 1 hour, turning lamb occasionally. Drain off marinade.
• Arrange lamb in ring in large shallow dish; cover with waxed paper and microwave at High for 3 minutes, turning dish twice. Turn and rearrange lamb. Cover and microwave at Medium (50%) for 1 to 3 minutes or until desired doneness. Let stand for 5 minutes. To serve, slice into 1/2-inch (1 cm) pieces. Makes 4 servings.

LAMB RACKS WITH HONEY-SOY GLAZE

Use this glaze for 8 lamb loin chops (about 1-1/2 lb/750 g total) in place of lamb racks.

1/4 cup	ketchup	50 mL
2 tbsp	honey	25 mL
1 tbsp	soy sauce	15 mL
1/2 tsp	minced gingerroot	2 mL
1	clove garlic, minced	1
2	racks of lamb (about 1-1/4 lb/ 600 g total)	2

• In large bowl, combine ketchup, honey, soy sauce, gingerroot and garlic; add lamb racks and turn to coat well.

• Arrange lamb on roasting rack with meatiest portions toward outside; brush with more of the glaze. Cover with waxed paper and microwave at High for 2 minutes.

• Turn racks over keeping thickest portions toward outside. Brush with remaining glaze. Microwave at Medium (50%) for 7 to 9 minutes or until firm to the touch and pink inside, rotating twice. Makes 4 servings.

LAMB CHOPS WITH PARSLEY

Lamb chops are ideal for a quick meal. Experiment with different herbs, such as basil and oregano, in the breading.

1-1/2 cups	fresh bread crumbs	375 mL
1/2 cup	chopped fresh parsley	125 mL
1	clove garlic, minced	1
1 tbsp	vegetable oil	15 mL
	Salt and pepper	
8	lamb chops (2 lb/ 1 kg total)	8

• Heat browning dish at High for 6 minutes or according to manufacturer's directions.
• Meanwhile, in small bowl, combine bread crumbs, parsley, garlic, oil, and salt and pepper to taste. Press mixture onto both sides of chops to coat completely.
• Place chops on hot browning dish and press down to brown meat; microwave at Medium (50%) for 6 minutes, turning chops halfway through cooking time. Makes 4 servings.

LAMB AND VEGETABLE NAVARIN

Give this delectable navarin a rich color by cooking the onions with a sprinkle of sugar and adding both tomatoes and tomato paste.

1	onion, chopped	1
1 tsp	granulated sugar	5 mL
2 lb	boneless lamb shoulder, cut in 1-inch (2.5 cm) cubes	1 kg
2 tbsp	all-purpose flour	25 mL
1	clove garlic, minced	1
1 tsp	butter	5 mL
1	can (14 oz/398 mL) tomatoes, chopped	1
1/2 cup	chicken stock	125 mL
1/2 cup	dry white wine or extra chicken stock	125 mL
2 tbsp	tomato paste	25 mL
1/2 tsp	pepper	2 mL
Pinch	each dried thyme and rosemary	Pinch
8	small potatoes, peeled and halved	8
3/4 cup	cubed rutabaga	175 mL
1-1/2 cups	sliced carrots	375 mL
3/4 cup	green beans, trimmed and halved	175 mL
1/2 cup	water	125 mL
	Salt and pepper	
1/4 cup	chopped fresh parsley	50 mL

• In 12-cup (3 L) casserole, sprinkle onion with sugar. Microwave at High for 8 to 10 minutes or until onion is lightly browned, stirring every 2 minutes.
• Toss lamb with flour; add to onion mixture along with garlic and butter. Cover and microwave at High for 10 minutes or until meat is evenly browned, stirring once. Stir in tomatoes, stock, wine, tomato paste, pepper, thyme and rosemary. Microwave at High, covered, for 5 minutes or until boiling. Stir; cover again. Microwave at Medium (50%) for 30 minutes or until meat is tender, stirring twice. Let stand, covered, for 10 to 12 minutes.
• Meanwhile, in 9-inch (23 cm) pie plate, arrange ring of potatoes around edge of dish, followed by ring of rutabaga, ring of carrots and mound of green beans. Pour water over vegetables; cover with vented plastic wrap and microwave at High for 10 to 12 minutes or until tender. Drain and stir into meat mixture. Season with salt and pepper to taste. Cover and microwave at High for 2 minutes or until heated through and flavors have blended. Sprinkle with parsley. Makes about 6 servings.

Lamb Racks with Honey-Soy Glaze

VEAL CHOPS WITH ORANGES

Depending on the season, use navel oranges, tangerines or clementines in this dish that's perfect for company.

1/2 cup	orange juice	125 mL
1/4 cup	dry white wine	50 mL
1 tbsp	cornstarch	15 mL
1 tbsp	packed brown sugar	15 mL
1 tbsp	orange marmalade ·	15 mL
1/4 tsp	dried mint (or 1 tbsp/15 mL chopped fresh)	1 mL
4	veal chops, well-trimmed (1-1/2 lb/ 750 g total)	4
	Pepper	
1 tsp	butter	5 mL
1 tsp	vegetable oil	5 mL
GARNISH:		
	Glazed Orange Slivers (recipe follows)	
	Orange slices	
	Fresh mint	

• Mix together orange juice, wine, cornstarch, sugar, marmalade and mint; set aside. Season chops with pepper to taste.

• Heat large browning skillet in microwave at High for 7 to 8 minutes or according to manufacturer's directions; add butter and oil. Quickly add chops and microwave at High for 2 minutes; pour off juices and turn chops over. Microwave at High for 3 minutes longer. Add orange juice mixture; cover with lid or vented plastic wrap and microwave at Medium (50%) for 10 minutes, rotating dish twice. Uncover and microwave at High for 3 to 5 minutes or until sauce thickens and chops are tender and cooked through, rotating dish twice.

• Garnish with Glazed Orange Slivers, orange slices and mint. Makes 4 servings.

GLAZED ORANGE SLIVERS:

1	large orange	1
3 tbsp	hot water	50 mL
1 tsp	granulated sugar	5 mL

• Remove zest (thin outer rind) from orange; cut into slivers and place in custard cup. Add 2 tbsp (25 mL) of the water; microwave at High for 1 minute; drain. Stir remaining water and sugar into dish; microwave at High for 1-1/2 to 2 minutes or until water has evaporated and slivers are glazed.

Veal Chops with Oranges

VEAL CHOPS AUX DUXELLES

Envelopes of moist tender veal chops with a tasty mushroom topping are fast and easy to prepare and impressive enough for company.

4	veal chops, about 1/2 inch (1 cm) thick (1-1/2 lb/ 750 g total), well-trimmed	4
	Pepper	
2 tsp	Dijon mustard	10 mL
1 tbsp	butter	15 mL
2 cups	coarsely chopped mushrooms	500 mL
1	small onion, chopped	1
1	clove garlic, minced	1
1/4 cup	chopped fresh parsley	50 mL

• Cut four 12- x 11-inch (30 x 28 cm) pieces of parchment paper; place 1 veal chop in center of each. Season chops with pepper to taste; evenly spread with mustard. Set aside.

• In 4-cup (1 L) measure, microwave butter at High for 30 seconds or until melted. Stir in mushrooms, onion and garlic; microwave at High, uncovered, for 2 to 4 minutes or until softened, stirring once. Pour off juices. Stir in parsley.

• Spoon mushroom mixture evenly over chops; wrap to form packages, sealing edges tightly. Slash tops to vent slightly. Arrange on large round plate with thickest portions toward outside of plate. Microwave at High for 5 minutes, rearranging after 3 minutes. Microwave at Medium (50%) for 8 to 12 minutes or until cooked through, rearranging after 5 minutes. Makes 4 servings.

VEAL SCALLOPINI ROLLS

Choose veal scallopini similar in size and shape for more even cooking.

2	veal scallopini (about 1/2 lb/250 g total)	2
1/3 cup	fresh bread crumbs	75 mL
3 tbsp	light mayonnaise	50 mL
2 tbsp	freshly grated Parmesan cheese	25 mL
1/2 tsp	grated lemon rind	2 mL
	Pepper	
4	spears asparagus	4
1 tbsp	butter	15 mL
2 tsp	chopped fresh parsley	10 mL

Apples and Pears with Cinnamon and Lemon is a quick and easy dessert (shown in our photograph). Core and slice 2 apples and 2 pears; arrange in a pie plate. Sprinkle with 2 tsp (10 mL) lemon juice and 1/2 tsp (2 mL) cinnamon; drizzle with 2 tbsp (25 mL) maple syrup. Cover with vented plastic wrap and microwave at High for 3 to 5 minutes or until fruit is tender. Serve warm or cold. Makes 4 servings.

Veal Chops aux Duxelles; Apples and Pears with Cinnamon and Lemon

• Pound scallopini to about 1/8-inch (3 mm) thickness; set aside.

• Mix together bread crumbs, mayonnaise, Parmesan, lemon rind, and pepper to taste; spread evenly over scallopini. Top each with 2 asparagus spears, trimmed to fit. Roll up each scallopini and secure with toothpick.

• In 8-inch (2 L) square dish, microwave butter at High for 30 to 45 seconds or until melted. Add scallopini rolls and cover with waxed paper; microwave at High for 1 minute. Turn rolls in butter; microwave at High for 1 minute. Reduce to Medium-High (70%) and microwave for 1 to 3 minutes or until meat is tender and no longer pink inside. Let stand for 5 minutes. Sprinkle with parsley. Makes 2 servings.

Poultry

At the end of a busy day, you can start by quickly defrosting chicken breasts and within a short time be serving a marvelous meal – thanks to your microwave and recipes like Californian Chicken (p. 82) or Chicken with Herbs and Mushrooms (p. 83). For fancier occasions, Chicken in a Pouch with Julienne Vegetables (p. 80) or Teriyaki Chicken (p. 27) fit the bill. Turkey Cordon Bleu Roll-Ups (p. 87) are perfect for a buffet dinner and Tandoori Cornish Hens (p. 86) make a spectacular entrée when finished on the barbecue.

CHICKEN VERONIQUE

Lightly glazed chicken bathed in grape-studded sauce is easy-to-make everyday fare that is also elegant enough for guests.

2-1/2 lb	chicken pieces	1.25 kg
1 tbsp	butter	15 mL
1 tbsp	olive oil	15 mL
1 tsp	browning sauce (optional)	5 mL
1/2 cup	marmalade	125 mL
1 cup	chicken stock	250 mL
3 tbsp	lemon juice	50 mL
1 tbsp	cornstarch	15 mL
1/2 cup	seedless green grapes, halved	125 mL
	Lemon slices	
	Parsley sprigs	

• Arrange chicken in shallow casserole dish, meatier portions toward outside. In small dish, microwave butter at High for 15 seconds or until melted; stir in oil, and browning sauce (if using). Brush over chicken; cover with waxed paper and microwave at High for 7 minutes, rotating dish twice; set aside.
• In small bowl, microwave marmalade at High for 30 seconds; spread half over chicken and set remaining marmalade aside. Cover chicken with waxed paper and microwave at High for 6 to 7 minutes or until chicken is tender, rotating dish once. Transfer to serving platter, reserving 2 tbsp (25 mL) pan drippings. Cover chicken with plastic wrap; let stand while preparing sauce.
• In 4-cup (1 L) measure or bowl, combine reserved pan drippings and chicken stock; microwave at High for 4 minutes or until boiling. Blend together lemon juice and cornstarch; stir into stock mixture. Microwave at High for 1 minute; stir in remaining marmalade. Taste and adjust seasoning if desired. Add grapes and microwave at High for 2 minutes. Pour sauce over chicken; garnish with lemon slices and parsley. Makes 4 to 6 servings.

TIPS FOR CHICKEN
• *All poultry should be defrosted for even cooking.*
• *Arrange chicken pieces in a single layer with thickest parts to outside of dish. Check partway through cooking; you may have to rearrange and turn pieces over.*
• *Shielding with aluminum foil may be necessary for wing tips and drumstick ends.*
• *To prevent bursting or popping skin on whole large birds or large pieces, prick in several places so juices and fat can be released.*
• *To prevent steaming the chicken and avoid oven spatters, cover poultry loosely with waxed paper while cooking.*
• *Remove skin of chicken pieces if you wish to remove excess fat between skin and meat. Chicken will cook more evenly and be juicy, but will not brown.*
• *To crisp skin on chicken pieces, partially cook chicken in the microwave then finish on the barbecue or under the broiler.*
• *When cooking crumb-coated chicken, place on a roasting rack or paper towel-lined baking dish, to keep from steaming and bubbling in drippings. Microwave, uncovered or lightly covered with paper towel.*

Chicken Veronique

CHICKEN IN A POUCH WITH JULIENNE VEGETABLES

Natural juices and flavors are retained when chicken breasts are tucked into parchment-paper pouches and quickly cooked in the microwave.

2 tbsp	butter	25 mL
4	boneless skinless chicken breasts (about 1 lb/500 g total)	4
4 tsp	Dijon mustard	20 mL
2	small carrots, thinly julienned	4
1	stalk celery, thinly julienned	1
1	leek (white part only), thinly julienned	1
1 tsp	dried thyme	5 mL
	Salt and pepper	

• Fold four 15- x 10-inch (35 x 25 cm) pieces of parchment paper in half crosswise; trim corners to form ovals. Open ovals and brush with butter, leaving 1-inch (2.5 cm) border around each.
• Place chicken breasts in center of one end of each oval; spread with mustard. Sprinkle evenly with carrots, celery, leek, thyme, and salt and pepper to taste.
• Fold paper over chicken and crimp edges to seal. Slash top to vent slightly. Arrange on large plate with thickest portions toward outside. Microwave at High for 6 to 8 minutes or until chicken is no longer pink inside, rotating halfway through. Let stand for 3 minutes before serving. Makes 4 servings.

Place chicken breast in the center of one end of the parchment paper oval.

If parchment paper is not available, use a large buttered pie plate. Position chicken pieces on plate with thickest parts to outside of dish. Spread with mustard, top with vegetables and seasonings. Cover with vented plastic wrap and microwave as directed in the recipe.

CHICKEN WITH TOMATOES AND PEPPERS

Here's a satisfying and zesty chicken dish with a Mediterranean flavor.

1-1/2 lb	chicken pieces	750 g
1 tbsp	olive oil	15 mL
1	onion, chopped	1
2	cloves garlic, minced	2
1 cup	chopped drained canned tomatoes	250 mL
3 tbsp	tomato paste	50 mL
2 tbsp	dry white wine	25 mL
1/2 tsp	dried oregano	2 mL
1/2 tsp	dried thyme	2 mL
1/2 tsp	granulated sugar	2 mL
Pinch	cayenne pepper	Pinch
	Salt and black pepper	
1	sweet green pepper, sliced	1
1	sweet red pepper, sliced	1
2 tbsp	chopped fresh parsley	25 mL

• Remove skin from chicken pieces; set aside.
• In 12-cup (3 L) casserole, combine oil, onion and garlic; microwave at High for 3 to 4 minutes or until softened. Add tomatoes, tomato paste, wine, oregano, thyme, sugar, cayenne, and salt and black pepper to taste. Cover and microwave at High for 5 to 7 minutes or until slightly thickened, stirring once.
• Add chicken pieces, spooning some sauce over top. Add green and red peppers; cover and microwave at High for 10 to 14 minutes or until chicken is no longer pink inside, stirring once. Sprinkle with parsley; let stand, covered, for 10 minutes. Makes 4 servings.

Chicken in a Pouch with Julienne Vegetables; Almond-Coated Warm Brie (p. 45)

CHICKEN TETRAZZINI

Enjoy chicken, mushrooms, celery and sweet pepper in a creamy wine-flavored sauce over spaghetti. Serve with a spinach salad and a slice of Carrot Cake (recipe, p. 141) for a down-home cozy meal. Turkey may be substituted for the chicken.

1/4 lb	spaghetti	125 g
1 tbsp	vegetable oil	15 mL
2 tbsp	butter	25 mL
1 cup	sliced mushrooms	250 mL
1/2 cup	diced celery	125 mL
1	onion, chopped	1
1/4 cup	diced sweet red or green pepper	50 mL
2 tbsp	all-purpose flour	25 mL
1 cup	chicken stock	250 mL
1/4 cup	light cream	50 mL
1/4 cup	dry white wine or milk	50 mL
3/4 tsp	salt	4 mL
Pinch	pepper	Pinch
2 cups	cubed cooked chicken	500 mL
2 tbsp	chopped fresh parsley	25 mL
1/4 cup	freshly grated Parmesan cheese	50 mL
1/4 cup	shredded Cheddar cheese	50 mL

• In large pot of boiling salted water, cook spaghetti until al dente (tender but firm). Drain, toss with oil and set aside.

• Meanwhile, in 8-cup (2 L) casserole, microwave butter at High for 30 seconds or until melted. Stir in mushrooms, celery and onion; microwave at High for 3 to 4 minutes or until tender, stirring once. Add sweet pepper; microwave at High for 1 minute.

• Stir in flour, stock, cream, wine, salt and pepper; microwave at High for 3-1/2 to 4-1/2 minutes or until mixture boils and thickens, stirring twice. Stir in chicken and parsley.

• Arrange spaghetti on serving platter. Spoon chicken mixture over pasta. Sprinkle with Parmesan and Cheddar cheeses. Serve immediately. If reheating is necessary, cover with waxed paper and microwave at Medium-High (70%) for 2 to 3 minutes or until hot. Makes 4 servings.

CHICKEN CACCIATORE

You can make this dish the night before and reheat it at serving time. Serve it over buttered egg noodles or hot fluffy rice (see p. 116).

1 cup	chopped celery	250 mL
1/2 cup	chopped onion	125 mL
1 tbsp	olive oil	15 mL
1	clove garlic, minced	1
3 tbsp	all-purpose flour	50 mL
1	can (28 oz/796 mL) tomatoes (undrained)	1
1 cup	sliced mushrooms	250 mL
1/2 cup	dry white wine or chicken stock	125 mL
1/4 cup	chopped fresh parsley	50 mL
2 tbsp	brandy (optional)	25 mL
1 tsp	each salt, paprika and dried oregano	5 mL
1	bay leaf	1
1/2 tsp	dried basil	2 mL
1/4 tsp	pepper	1 mL
4	chicken breasts (2 lb/1 kg total), skinned	4

• In 12-cup (3 L) casserole, combine celery, onion, oil and garlic. Microwave at High for 3-1/2 to 4-1/2 minutes or until vegetables are tender, stirring once.
• Blend in flour until vegetables are coated; stir in tomatoes, breaking up with fork. Stir in mushrooms, wine, parsley, brandy (if using), salt, paprika, oregano, bay leaf, basil and pepper. Cover and microwave at High for 5 minutes, stirring once. Remove bay leaf.
• Add chicken to casserole, arranging thick portions toward outside of dish. Cover and microwave at High for 25 to 30 minutes or until chicken is no longer pink, rotating dish once. Let stand for 5 minutes before serving. Makes 4 servings.

CALIFORNIAN CHICKEN

Try this up-to-date chicken, with lime juice, avocado and jalapeño pepper adding that California style.

4	boneless chicken breasts (1 lb/500 g total)	4
1	tomato, chopped	1
2 tbsp	finely chopped onion	25 mL
1 tbsp	lime juice	15 mL
1 tsp	chopped pickled jalapeño pepper	5 mL
Half	avocado, sliced	Half
1 tbsp	chopped fresh parsley or coriander	15 mL
	Salt and pepper	

• Arrange chicken in pie plate with thickest portions toward outside; sprinkle with tomato, onion, lime juice and jalapeño pepper.
• Cover with waxed paper and microwave at High for 7 to 9 minutes or until chicken is no longer pink inside, rotating dish twice. Arrange avocado on top and sprinkle with parsley; let stand, covered, for 2 minutes. Season with salt and pepper to taste. Makes 4 servings.

DEFROSTING CHICKEN

• *To defrost chicken pieces: Remove chicken from wrapping or heat will build up inside packaging and start to cook the outside before the inside has thawed. Place on rack in cooking dish, to allow juices to drain. Cover with vented plastic wrap.*
• *Microwave chicken pieces at Medium-Low (30%), allowing 14 to 16 minutes for each 2-1/2 to 3 pounds (1.5 kg) of chicken.*
• *Rearrange and remove pieces as they thaw.*
• *To defrost a whole chicken: Remove chicken from wrapping and remove metal clips, if necessary. Allow 10 to 12 minutes per pound (20 to 24 minutes per kg). Wing tips and drumsticks may require shielding to prevent the start of cooking during defrosting time.*

COOKING CHICKEN

• *To cook a whole chicken, tie legs together and tuck wing tips under. Place bird breast side down on microwaveable roasting rack or inverted saucer. This keeps bird above cooking juices and avoids a steamed flavor.*
• *Cooking times for whole chicken cooked at High are:*
11 to 15 min. 2 lb (1 kg)
25 to 26 min. 4 lb (2 kg)
36 to 38 min. 6 lb (3 kg)
• *Turn bird over halfway through cooking time.*
• *Test for doneness after standing time.*
• *Cook chicken pieces, covered, at High for 6 to 8 minutes per pound (500 g). Turn and rearrange pieces at least once during cooking.*

(Clockwise from top right)
Californian Chicken;
Fish with Peppers and
Parsley (p. 94); Chicken
with Herbs and Mush-
rooms; Fish with Gin-
gered Pineapple (p. 95)

CHICKEN WITH HERBS AND MUSHROOMS

*Boneless chicken breasts are one of the
simplest, fastest meats to cook. Dijon mustard,
white wine and mushrooms add a sophisticated
French flair.*

4	boneless chicken breasts (1 lb/500 g total)	4
2 tsp	Dijon mustard	10 mL
1 cup	sliced mushrooms	250 mL
1 tbsp	white wine	15 mL
1 tbsp	chopped fresh thyme (or 1/2 tsp/ 2 mL dried)	15 mL
2 tbsp	freshly grated Parmesan cheese	25 mL
	Salt and pepper	

• Arrange chicken in pie plate with thickest
portions toward outside. Spread with
mustard; sprinkle with mushrooms, wine
and thyme.
• Cover with waxed paper and microwave at
High for 7 to 9 minutes or until chicken is
no longer pink inside, rotating dish twice.
Sprinkle with Parmesan; let stand, covered
for 2 minutes. Season with salt and pepper
to taste. Makes 4 servings.

CHICKEN BROCHETTE WITH SAGE LEMON BUTTER

The Sage Lemon Butter, a snap to make in the microwave, gives the chicken brochette a zesty piquant taste.

1 lb	boneless, skinless chicken breasts	500 g
1 tbsp	each lemon juice and olive oil	15 mL
1	clove garlic, minced	1
2 tsp	crumbled dried sage	10 mL
1/2 tsp	pepper	2 mL
3 oz	thinly sliced Black Forest or prosciutto ham	75 g
	Sage Lemon Butter (recipe follows)	

• Cut chicken into 1-1/2-inch (4 cm) cubes. In large bowl, whisk together lemon juice, oil, garlic, sage and pepper. Add chicken; toss to coat and let stand 10 minutes.
• Cut ham into strips approximately 1-1/2 inches (4 cm) wide. Thread chicken onto 4 oiled wooden skewers, lacing ham around and between chicken pieces. Arrange skewers on plate, like spokes in a wheel, if possible, or in a row. Do not pack brochettes tightly. Microwave at High, uncovered, for 4 to 6 minutes, or until chicken is no longer pink inside, turning and rearranging brochettes every 2 minutes. To serve, slip chicken off skewers onto plates and pass Sage Lemon Butter separately. Makes 4 servings.

SAGE LEMON BUTTER:

1/2 cup	butter	125 mL
2 tsp	lemon juice	10 mL
1 tsp	crumbled dried sage	5 mL
1/2 tsp	grated lemon rind	2 mL
	Salt and pepper	

• In small bowl, microwave butter at Medium-Low (30%), for 30 to 40 seconds, or just until softened. Add lemon juice, sage, lemon rind, and salt and pepper to taste; whisk until smooth. Makes about 1/2 cup (125 mL).

Compound butters, such as Sage Lemon Butter, are made by flavoring softened butter with herbs, mustard, lemon juice, wine or other seasonings. These butters complement meat, fish, poultry or vegetable dishes. The microwave oven is a great tool for making these quickly because the butter must be softened, not melted. To soften 1/2 cup (125 mL) butter, microwave at Medium-Low (30%) for 20 to 40 seconds, watching carefully.

SUNDAY CHICKEN

Sunday once meant roast chicken for dinner. Instead, try this whole chicken, combined with the tang of orange and apricot, for a change. Serve with Brussels Sprouts with Toasted Almonds (recipe, p. 128) for a modern Sunday meal.

1	chicken (3 lb/ 1.5 kg)	1
	Salt and pepper	
1	orange (unpeeled), quartered	1
2 tsp	dry mustard	10 mL
2 tbsp	apricot jam or chutney	25 mL
2 tbsp	soy sauce	25 mL
1 tbsp	water	15 mL
2 tsp	cornstarch	10 mL

• Pat chicken dry inside and out. Sprinkle cavity with salt and pepper to taste; insert orange quarters. Tuck wing tips behind back and tie legs together with string.
• Pat mustard over chicken. Combine jam with soy sauce; brush over chicken. Place breast side down on rack or inverted saucer in greased 11- x 7-inch (2 L) baking dish. Cover with waxed paper and microwave at High for 10 minutes. Turn chicken over; baste with pan juices. Microwave at Medium (50%) for 20 to 30 minutes or until juices run clear when chicken is pierced with fork, basting and rotating dish twice. Transfer to serving platter; cover and let stand for 10 minutes.
• Strain pan juices into 2-cup (500 mL) measure; skim off fat. Blend water with cornstarch; stir into juices. Microwave at High for 1 to 2 minutes or until thickened and smooth, stirring twice. Makes 4 servings.

Place the bird breast side down in a baking dish.

Sunday Chicken; Brussels Sprouts with Toasted Almonds (p. 128)

CHICKEN FINGERS

Here's a delicious way to enjoy fast food at home.

1 lb	boneless skinless chicken breasts	500 g
1/4 cup	(approx) all-purpose flour	50 mL
2	eggs, beaten	2
	Chicken Coating Mix (recipe follows)	
3 tbsp	butter, melted	50 mL

CHICKEN COATING MIX:

3/4 cup	fine dry bread crumbs	175 mL
2 tsp	paprika	10 mL
1/4 tsp	dried thyme	1 mL
Half	small bay leaf	Half

• Cut chicken into 2-inch (5 cm) strips about 1/2 inch wide; pat dry with paper towels. Place flour in shallow dish, eggs in another and coating mix in a third. Dip chicken pieces into flour; shake off excess. Dip into eggs; allow excess to drip off. Firmly press into coating mix.
• Arrange breaded chicken pieces in circle on 10-inch (25 cm) round platter with thicker portions toward outside. Drizzle with melted butter. Cover with paper towel.
• Microwave at High for 4-1/2 to 5-1/2 minutes or until no longer pink inside. Let stand for 5 minutes. Makes 4 servings.

• In blender or food processor, combine bread crumbs, paprika, thyme and bay leaf; process until bay leaf is ground to fine powder. Store in refrigerator. Makes about 3/4 cup (175 mL).

TANDOORI CORNISH HENS

For a browner, crispier skin, split hens after standing time, then broil for 3 to 5 minutes or until desired color. This is an excellent recipe for precooking in the microwave then finishing on the barbecue.

2	Cornish hens (about 1-1/2 lb/ 750 g each)	2
2 tbsp	lemon juice	25 mL
1 tbsp	finely chopped gingerroot	15 mL
1 tsp	turmeric	5 mL
1 tsp	paprika	5 mL
1/2 tsp	ground coriander	2 mL
1/4 tsp	cayenne pepper	1 mL
1/4 tsp	cinnamon	1 mL
1	clove garlic, chopped	1
1/2 cup	sour cream or yogurt	125 mL
	Salt	

• Rinse hens and pat dry inside and out with paper towels. Combine lemon juice, gingerroot, turmeric, paprika, coriander, cayenne pepper, cinnamon and garlic; stir into sour cream. Pour over hens in plastic bag or large bowl, turning to coat hens all over. Cover and refrigerate for 8 hours or overnight, turning several times.
• Place hens, breast sides down, in shallow oval or rectangular dish. Brush with marinade; cover with waxed paper and microwave at High for 8 minutes, rotating dish once.
• Turn hens over; brush with marinade. Cover with waxed paper and microwave at Medium-High (70%) for 8 minutes, rotating dish once. (If finishing hens under broiler or on grill, remove and let stand for 10 minutes before finishing.)
• If not broiling or grilling, microwave at High for 2 to 4 minutes longer or until thigh is no longer pink near bone when tested with knife. Let stand for 10 minutes. Season lightly with salt. To serve: Cut hens in two, using poultry shears or sharp knife, discarding backbone. Makes 4 servings.

To make dried bread crumbs, place 5 slices whole wheat bread in a circle on double thickness of paper towels. Microwave at High for 3 minutes. Turn bread over; rearrange slices and microwave at High for 2 to 3 minutes longer or until dry. Process in blender or food processor. Makes about 3/4 cup (175 mL) crumbs.

Turkey Cordon Bleu Roll-Ups

TURKEY CORDON BLEU ROLL-UPS

This elegant casserole combines succulent Black Forest Ham with turkey scallopini. Ideal for a buffet dinner.

2/3 cup	dry bread crumbs	150 mL
1/2 tsp	dried thyme	2 mL
Pinch	pepper	Pinch
4	thin slices Black Forest ham (about 1/4 lb/125 g total)	4
1 lb	turkey or chicken scallopini*	500 g
2 tsp	Dijon mustard	10 mL
2 oz	Swiss cheese	50 g
1	egg, lightly beaten	1
	Cherry or yellow teardrop tomatoes	

• In pie plate, combine bread crumbs, thyme, and pepper; microwave at High, uncovered, for 2 to 3 minutes or until toasted, stirring every minute. Set aside.

• Arrange 1 slice of ham over each of 4 slices of turkey; spread mustard evenly over ham. Cut cheese into 12 pieces; place 3 pieces on top of each ham slice. Fold in sides of turkey and roll up.

• Place egg in shallow dish; dip turkey rolls into egg, coating well. Dip into bread crumbs, coating all over. Arrange on round serving dish like spokes of a wheel; cover with waxed paper and microwave at Medium (50%) for 8 to 10 minutes or until turkey is no longer pink, rotating dish twice. Let stand for 3 minutes. Garnish with tomatoes. Makes 4 servings.

*Between waxed paper, pound chicken breasts or 1/4-inch (5 mm) thick slices of turkey breast to 1/8-inch (3 mm) thickness.

GLAZED TURKEY BREAST

Make 6 regular servings from this amount of turkey or use 4 servings and have enough turkey left to make Hot Turkey Sandwiches (recipe, p. 90).

1-3/4 lb	boneless skinless turkey breast	875 g
1 tsp	paprika	5 mL
Pinch	cayenne pepper	Pinch
2 tbsp	orange marmalade	25 mL
4 tsp	Dijon mustard	20 mL

• Between 2 sheets of waxed paper, pound turkey slightly. Fold thin parts of breast under, envelope style; secure with 3 toothpicks, making an even thickness of meat.

• Combine paprika and cayenne pepper; sprinkle about half of the mixture over underside of breast. Place coated side up on roasting rack or in 8-inch (2 L) square baking dish resting on inverted saucer. Cover with waxed paper and microwave at High for 4 minutes.

• Turn breast over. Pat on remaining paprika mixture. Cover with waxed paper and microwave at Medium (50%) for 10 minutes, rotating rack twice.

• Combine marmalade and mustard; brush all over breast. Shield ends with foil if necessary; microwave at Medium (50%) for 7 to 10 minutes or until juices run clear when turkey is pierced with fork, rotating dish twice.

• Tent with foil and let stand for 10 minutes. To serve, remove toothpicks and cut into thin slices. Makes 8 servings.

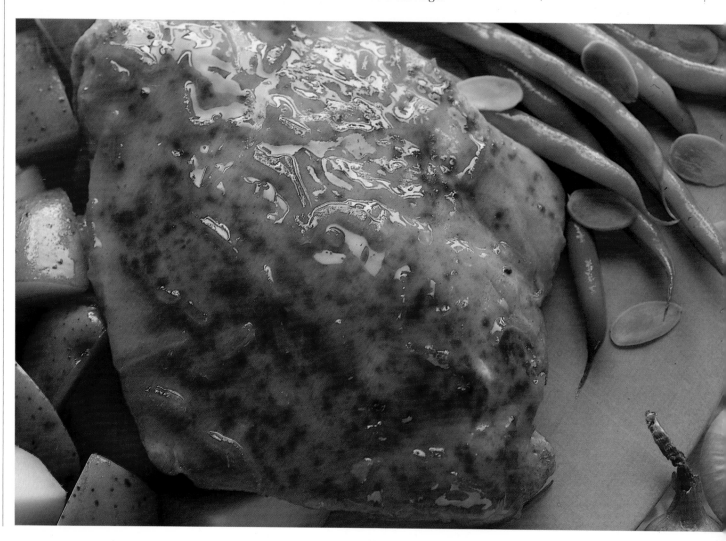

BARBECUED TURKEY

The microwave-plus-barbecue-rotisserie method of cooking a whole turkey retains so much of the juices you'll never "just barbecue" poultry again. A 10-lb (4.5 kg) turkey is the ideal size to fit in both a microwave oven and on a barbecue rotisserie.

1	turkey (10 lb/4.5 kg)	1
1 tsp	salt	5 mL
1/2 tsp	pepper	2 mL
2	slices orange (each 1/2-inch/1 cm thick)	2
1	onion, quartered	1
1	stalk celery (with leaves), quartered	1
MARINADE:		
1/4 cup	liquid honey	50 mL
1/2 cup	soy sauce	125 mL
1 tbsp	chopped fresh thyme (or 1 tsp/ 5 mL dried)	15 mL
1 tbsp	finely chopped gingerroot (or 1 tsp/5 mL ground ginger)	15 mL
1	clove garlic, minced	1

Glazed Turkey Breast

• Remove giblets from turkey and reserve for some other use; remove and discard excess fat and any metal clamps from turkey. Rinse cavity of turkey and pat dry. Sprinkle cavity with salt and pepper; loosely stuff with orange slices, onion and celery. Sew openings closed with string, or skewer with wooden toothpicks. Tie legs and wings close to body with string. Place turkey breast side up on roasting rack or in large baking dish.

• **Marinade:** In 2-cup (500 mL) measure, mix together honey, soy sauce, thyme, gingerroot and garlic. Brush over turkey, reserving remaining marinade. Wrap tips of wings and legs with small pieces of foil to prevent overcooking.

• Cover loosely with waxed paper. Microwave at High for 10 minutes. Turn turkey breast side down; baste with sauce. Cover and microwave at Medium (50%) for 25 minutes, rotating dish twice. Drain off any drippings. Turn breast side up and re-cover. Microwave at Medium (50%) for 25 minutes, rotating dish twice. Remove waxed paper and foil.

• Meanwhile, remove grills from barbecue. When coals are hot, arrange toward outside of firebox. Place drip pan in center to catch drippings.

• Re-tie turkey if trussing is loose. Insert rotisserie spit lengthwise through turkey and place over medium coals. Baste turkey with reserved marinade. Close barbecue lid. Grill turkey, basting occasionally, for 35 to 45 minutes or until thermometer registers 185°F (85°C) when inserted in meaty part of thigh or juices run clear. Remove turkey from spit; transfer to warm serving platter. Cover loosely with foil; let stand for 10 to 15 minutes before carving. Makes about 12 servings.

HOT TURKEY SANDWICH

Eat this hearty, open-faced sandwich with a knife and fork.

2	large crusty rolls	2
	Butter	
1/2 lb	sliced cooked turkey	250 g
Half	avocado, peeled and sliced	Half
1	tomato, seeded and chopped	1
3	green onions, chopped	3
1/2 cup	mayonnaise	125 mL
1/4 tsp	Worcestershire sauce	1 mL
Dash	hot pepper sauce	Dash
1/4 tsp	salt	1 mL
1/4 tsp	pepper	1 mL
2 cups	shredded Cheddar cheese	500 mL

• Slice rolls in half horizontally and lightly butter; arrange in circle on large round plate. Top each with turkey, then with avocado. Reserve 2 tbsp (25 mL) tomato for garnish; sprinkle remaining tomato and onion over avocado.

• In bowl, combine mayonnaise, Worcestershire sauce, hot pepper sauce, salt and pepper; stir in cheese. Top each sandwich with cheese mixture; microwave, uncovered, at Medium (50%) for 5 to 7 minutes or until cheese melts. Garnish with reserved tomato. Makes 4 servings.

MICROWAVING A WHOLE TURKEY

• *Stuff turkey with your favorite dressing. Tie legs after closing cavity; tuck wing tips under. Stuffing does not add to cooking time in the microwave oven.*

• *Wing tips and drumsticks may require shielding with smooth pieces of foil. Be sure foil is at least 1 inch (2.5 cm) away from oven walls to prevent arcing.*

• *Start turkey breast side down on a rack placed in a deep dish. Turkeys take about 12 to 15 minutes per pound (25 to 35 minutes per kg) to cook. Microwave at High for 10 minutes, then at Medium (50%) for remaining time.*

• *Turn bird over halfway through cooking time. Baste with a browning mixture* or pan juices occasionally; rotate dish several times.*

• *Pour drippings from bottom of dish into a large measuring cup or container for making gravy. (Leaving them in increases cooking time.)*

• *After cooking, let stand, tented with foil, for 20 minutes.*

• *For crisp skin, finish the bird in your conventional oven or on the barbecue.*

* Turkeys will brown in the oven, but a basting mixture of melted butter and paprika or a browning sauce improves the color. The Canadian Turkey Marketing Agency recommends brushing turkey halfway through cooking with a browning mixture made by combining 1 egg yolk, 1 tbsp (15 mL) vegetable oil and 1 to 2 tsp (5 to 10 mL) browning sauce like soy or teriyaki sauce.

Hot Turkey Sandwich

Fish and Seafood

Cooking fish and seafood is one of the things the microwave oven does best. With microwave cooking, fish is done in minutes and stays moist and tender throughout. Try Fish with Peppers and Parsley (p. 94) or Fish with Gingered Pineapple (p. 95), for starters. Once you've tried them, you may never cook fish any other way. For unexpected guests, Sole Fillets with Mushroom-Tomato Cream Sauce (p. 101) or Whole Fish with Rice Stuffing (p. 102) are the quick but elegant answer. Clams and Mussels with Wine and Herbs (p. 103) are delicious as either an appetizer or a main course.

CREOLE FISH STEW

This zesty, aromatic supper in a bowl only looks and tastes expensive. You can take advantage of supermarket specials and use any white fish you like.

2	onions, chopped	2
2	stalks celery, chopped	2
2	cloves garlic, minced	2
2 tbsp	vegetable oil	25 mL
1/4 cup	all-purpose flour	50 mL
3 cups	chicken stock	750 mL
1	can (28 oz/796 mL) tomatoes (undrained), coarsely chopped	1
1/4 cup	coarsely chopped fresh parsley	50 mL
1 tsp	each dried oregano and marjoram	5 mL
1 tsp	salt	5 mL
1/4 tsp	pepper	1 mL
1	bay leaf	1
1 lb	fish fillets, cut in 1-inch (2.5 cm) cubes	500 g

• In 12-cup (3 L) casserole, combine onions, celery, garlic and oil. Microwave at High for 6 to 8 minutes or until vegetables are tender, stirring twice.
• Stir in flour. Microwave at High for 1 minute; stir well. Stir in stock, tomatoes, parsley, oregano, marjoram, salt, pepper and bay leaf. Microwave, covered, at High for 12 to 14 minutes or until bubbly, stirring once.
• Stir in fish. Microwave, covered, at High for 10 to 12 minutes or until fish flakes when tested with fork, stirring once. Remove bay leaf. Makes 6 servings.

Teriyaki Salmon Chunks

TERIYAKI SALMON CHUNKS

Cook just before serving for a hot salmon salad, or cook ahead of time and chill for a delicious summer dish. Four small salmon steaks (about 1-1/4 lb/625 g) may be used in place of the fillet.

1/3 cup	teriyaki sauce	75 mL
2 tbsp	vegetable oil	25 mL
1 tbsp	chopped gingerroot	15 mL
1 tbsp	lemon juice	15 mL
1 lb	salmon fillet	500 g

• In shallow dish, combine teriyaki sauce, oil, gingerroot and lemon juice. Add salmon and marinate in refrigerator for at least 2 hours or overnight for stronger flavor, turning salmon several times.

• Drain marinade from salmon. Cover with vented plastic wrap and microwave at High for 4 to 5 minutes or just until barely opaque, rotating dish once. Let stand for 5 minutes. (If cooking steaks, place thickest ends toward outside of dish.) Makes about 4 servings.

FISH WITH PEPPERS AND PARSLEY

Julienned sweet red and green peppers add a colorful touch to this simple fish dish (photo, p. 83).

1	pkg (1 lb/500 g) frozen fish fillets, thawed (haddock, cod, Boston bluefish)	1
1 cup	julienned sweet red and green peppers	250 mL
2 tbsp	finely chopped onion	25 mL
1 tbsp	white wine	15 mL
1 tbsp	chopped fresh basil (or 1 tsp/5 mL dry)	15 mL
	Salt and pepper	
2 tbsp	freshly grated Parmesan cheese	25 mL
1 tbsp	chopped fresh parsley	15 mL

• Cut block of fish fillets into 4 equal pieces; arrange like spokes in a wheel on pie plate.
• Sprinkle fish with red and green pepper strips, onion, wine and basil. Cover with waxed paper and microwave at High for 5 to 7 minutes or until fish is opaque, rotating dish twice.
• Season with salt and pepper to taste; sprinkle with Parmesan and parsley. Let stand, covered, for 5 minutes. Makes 4 servings.

TIPS FOR FISH
• *Fish should be fresh or thawed before cooking, unless otherwise specified in recipe.*

TO DEFROST FISH
• *Remove fish from wrapping or heat will build up inside packaging and start to cook the outside before the inside is thawed. Place on rack in cooking dish, to allow juices to drain. Cover.*
• *Microwave at Medium-Low (30%):*
fillets — 5 to 6 minutes per lb (500 g)
whole fish — 5 to 8 minutes per 1-1/2 lb (750 g).
• *Halfway through defrosting time,*

Tuna Casserole

separate individual pieces or fillets, arranging icier pieces toward outside of dish. Turn over whole fish. Shield any warm spots with foil or remove pieces that feel cold and pliable. Cold, running water will help to separate fillets.

• Let fillets stand for 10 minutes, whole fish for 15 to 30 minutes, before cooking, to defrost completely.

TO COOK FISH

• *Arrange fish with thickest portions toward outside of dish or fold thin ends of fillets over to make a thicker, more uniform fillet for even cooking.*

• *Cook fish fillets or sticks in one layer in dish, preferably in circular pattern. Rearrange halfway through cooking time if necessary.*

• *Cover with lid or vented plastic wrap.*

• *When cooking crumb or nut coated fish, place coated fish pieces on roasting rack or paper towel-lined plate. Microwave, uncovered or lightly covered with paper towel.*

• *Fish and shellfish are naturally tender and require very little cooking. Overcooking toughens and dries seafood.*

• *Microwave at High: fillets — 4 to 6 minutes per lb (500 g) whole fish — 5 to 8 minutes per lb (500 g)*

• *Microwave at Medium (50%): salmon steaks — 6 to 8 minutes per lb (500 g)*

• *Let stand for 5 minutes after cooking.*

TUNA CASSEROLE

A new twist to an old favorite. Stir tender-crisp broccoli florets into the casserole, add a crunchy topping, and you have a meal-in-a-dish.

3 tbsp	butter	50 mL
1/2 cup	chopped celery	125 mL
1/2 cup	chopped green onion	125 mL
1	clove garlic, minced	1
1/4 cup	all-purpose flour	50 mL
2-1/2 cups	milk	625 mL
1 cup	shredded Swiss cheese	250 mL
1/4 tsp	dry mustard	1 mL
1/3 cup	sour cream	75 mL
	Salt and pepper	
2 cups	broccoli florets, cut in bite-size pieces	500 mL
2 tbsp	water	25 mL
Half	pkg egg noodles (375 g pkg), cooked	Half
2	cans (7 oz/198 g each) tuna, drained and flaked	2

TOPPING:		
1/2 cup	shredded Swiss cheese	125 mL
1/3 cup	whole wheat cracker crumbs	75 mL
2 tbsp	butter, melted	25 mL

• In 12-cup (3 L) dish, microwave butter at High for 30 seconds or until melted. Stir in celery, onions and garlic; microwave at High for 3 minutes or until softened, stirring once.

• Stir in flour until well blended; gradually stir in milk. Microwave, uncovered, at High for 6 to 8 minutes or until thickened, whisking 3 times. Stir in cheese and mustard until cheese has melted. Stir in sour cream; season with salt and pepper to taste. Cover and keep warm.

• Meanwhile, arrange broccoli around outside of large dish with stalks toward rim. Sprinkle with water; cover with vented plastic wrap and microwave at High for 2 minutes or until tender-crisp. Drain well.

• Stir broccoli into cheese sauce along with cooked noodles and tuna. Cover and microwave at Medium-High (70%) for 8 to 10 minutes or until heated through, stirring twice.

• **Topping:** Combine Swiss cheese, cracker crumbs and butter; sprinkle over casserole. Microwave, uncovered, at Medium-High (70%) for 2 minutes or until cheese has melted. Makes about 6 servings.

FISH WITH GINGERED PINEAPPLE

Simple fish fillets are given an Oriental flavor (photo, p. 83).

1	pkg (1 lb/500 g) frozen fish fillets, thawed (haddock, cod, Boston bluefish)	1
2 tsp	hoisin sauce	10 mL
1 tbsp	soy sauce	15 mL
2 tsp	sherry	10 mL
1 tsp	minced gingerroot	5 mL
1	green onion, sliced	1
1 cup	drained crushed pineapple	250 mL
	Salt and pepper	

• Cut block of fish fillets into 4 equal pieces; arrange like spokes in a wheel on pie plate.

• Spread fish with hoisin sauce; sprinkle with soy sauce, sherry, gingerroot and green onion. Spoon pineapple evenly onto pieces.

• Cover with waxed paper and microwave at High for 5 to 7 minutes or until fish is opaque, rotating plate twice. Season with salt and pepper to taste. Let stand, covered, for 5 minutes. Makes 4 servings.

HOMEMADE FISH STICKS

If you own a browning grill, this is the time to use it. Though both of these cooking methods work well, the browning grill gives the fish sticks a delicious crisp coating. Serve with Cucumber Sauce (recipe, p. 159).

1	pkg (1 lb/500 g) frozen white fish (sole, haddock, cod or Boston bluefish)	1
1/4 cup	dry bread crumbs	50 mL
1/4 cup	wheat germ	50 mL
1/4 cup	sesame seeds	50 mL
1 tsp	paprika	5 mL
1/4 tsp	salt	1 mL
	Pepper	
1	egg	1
1 tbsp	vegetable oil	15 mL

- Remove wrapping from fish. In shallow dish, thaw at Medium-Low (30%) for 2 to 3 minutes or just until fish can be cut with knife. Do not separate into fillets. Cut crosswise into 8 even sticks.
- In shallow dish, combine bread crumbs, wheat germ, sesame seeds, paprika, salt, and pepper to taste. In bowl, beat together egg and oil. Roll fish sticks in bread crumb mixture, then in egg mixture and again in bread crumb mixture.
- Heat browning dish at High for 4 minutes or according to manufacturer's directions. Brush dish with oil. Arrange fish sticks in dish like spokes in a wheel. Microwave at High for 1-1/2 minutes; turn fish over. Microwave at High for 2 to 3 minutes or until fish is opaque and flakes easily when tested with fork.
- Alternatively, on roasting rack, arrange fish like spokes in a wheel. Microwave at High for 5 to 6 minutes or until fish is opaque and flakes easily when tested with fork, rotating dish once during cooking. Makes 4 servings.

HALIBUT WITH TOMATO SAUCE

Moist tender fish served with chunky tomato sauce is quick and easy to make for a dinner the whole family will love. Serve with hot egg noodles tossed with butter and grated Parmesan cheese.

1 tbsp	vegetable oil	15 mL
1	clove garlic, minced	1
1	onion, chopped	1
1/3 cup	diced zucchini	75 mL
1/3 cup	chopped celery	75 mL
1/3 cup	chopped sweet green pepper	75 mL
1	can (7-1/2 oz/ 213 mL) tomato sauce	1
1/2 tsp	dried basil	2 mL
1/2 tsp	dried oregano	2 mL
1/2 tsp	granulated sugar	2 mL
1 tbsp	butter	15 mL
1 tbsp	lemon juice	15 mL
4	halibut steaks (1-1/2 lb/750 g total)	4
	Salt and pepper	

- In 4-cup (1 L) measure, combine oil, garlic and onion; microwave at High for 2 to 3 minutes or until softened.
- Stir in zucchini, celery and green pepper; cover with vented plastic wrap and microwave at High for 3 to 5 minutes or until softened, stirring once.
- Stir in tomato sauce, basil, oregano and sugar; microwave, covered, at High for 3 to 5 minutes or until heated through, stirring once. Set aside while cooking fish.
- In large shallow round dish, microwave butter at High for 30 seconds or until melted; stir in lemon juice. Arrange fish on dish, thickest portions toward outside. Cover with vented plastic wrap and microwave at High for 3 minutes; rearrange fish and rotate dish. Microwave at High for 1 to 4 minutes or until just opaque, rotating dish once. Let stand, covered, for 5 minutes.
- Reheat sauce, covered, at High for 3 to 5 minutes or until heated through. Season with salt and pepper to taste. Arrange fish on serving plates and pour sauce over. Makes 4 servings.

Halibut with Tomato Sauce

FISH WITH MUSHROOMS AND BASIL

White wine, mushrooms and pine nuts make this fish dish special.

1	pkg (1 lb/500 g) frozen fish fillets, thawed (haddock, cod, Boston bluefish)	1
1 tbsp	white wine	15 mL
1 cup	sliced mushrooms	250 mL
2	green onions, julienned	2
1 tbsp	chopped fresh basil (or 1 tsp/5 mL dried)	15 mL
	Salt and pepper	
2 tbsp	toasted pine nuts*	25 mL

• Cut block of fish fillets into 4 equal pieces; arrange like spokes in a wheel on pie plate.
• Sprinkle fish with wine, then mushrooms, onions and basil. Cover with waxed paper and microwave at High for 5 to 7 minutes or until fish is opaque, rotating plate twice.
• Season with salt and pepper to taste; garnish with pine nuts. Let stand, covered, for 5 minutes. Makes 4 servings.
*To toast pine nuts, spread in pie plate and microwave at High for 2 to 4 minutes or until toasted, stirring every 30 seconds.

SALMON RING WITH HOT MAYONNAISE SAUCE

When company arrives, whip up this elegant salmon dish. For a festive look, spoon colorful Almond Rice Pilaf (recipe, p. 122) in the center of the ring. A tangy, rich Lemon Curd Pie (recipe, p. 149) is the ideal finishing touch.

1	can (15 oz/426 g) red salmon, drained and flaked	1
1/2 cup	each finely chopped celery and onion	125 mL
1/2 cup	mayonnaise	125 mL
1	egg, lightly beaten	1
1/4 cup	dry bread crumbs or finely crushed soda crackers	50 mL
1 tsp	dried dillweed	5 mL
1 tbsp	lemon juice	15 mL
1/2 tsp	each dry mustard and salt	2 mL
1/4 tsp	pepper	1 mL
SAUCE:		
1/2 cup	each mayonnaise and plain yogurt	125 mL
1 tbsp	drained capers	15 mL
2 tsp	horseradish	10 mL
2 tsp	coarse grainy mustard	10 mL
1 tsp	lemon juice	5 mL

• Combine salmon, celery, onion, mayonnaise, egg, bread crumbs, dill, lemon juice, mustard, salt and 1/4 tsp (1 mL) pepper. Press into greased 4-cup (1 L) ring mould; cover with vented plastic wrap. Microwave at High for 4 to 6 minutes or until firm to the touch. Let stand, covered, for 5 minutes.
• **Sauce:** In 2-cup (500 mL) measure, combine mayonnaise, yogurt, capers, horseradish, mustard and lemon juice; stir until smooth. Microwave at High for 30 to 60 seconds or just until heated through. Invert salmon ring onto platter and serve with sauce. Makes 4 servings.

Salmon Ring with Hot Mayonnaise Sauce; Almond Rice Pilaf (p. 122); Lemon Curd Pie (p. 149)

FISH WITH CUCUMBER AND CAPERS

Cucumber, onion and dill bring a change of flavor to an everyday fish dish; capers add an unusual touch.

1	pkg (1 lb/500 g) frozen fish fillets, thawed (haddock, cod, Boston bluefish)	1
1 tbsp	lemon juice	15 mL
1 cup	thinly sliced peeled cucumber	250 mL
1 tbsp	minced onion	15 mL
1 tbsp	chopped capers	15 mL
1 tbsp	chopped fresh dill	15 mL
1/2 tsp	grated lemon rind	2 mL
	Salt and pepper	

• Cut block of fish fillets into 4 equal pieces; arrange like spokes in a wheel on pie plate.
• Sprinkle fish with lemon juice, then with cucumber, onion, capers, dill and lemon rind. Cover with waxed paper and microwave at High for 5 to 7 minutes or until fish is opaque, rotating plate twice.
• Season with salt and pepper to taste. Let stand, covered, for 5 minutes. Makes 4 servings.

ORIENTAL WHOLE FISH

For an Oriental-style fish dinner, serve this on a bed of micro-steamed rice (sidebar, p. 116) and have Mini-Mandarin Cheesecakes (recipe, p. 155) ready for dessert.

2 lb	whole fish (salmon trout, lake trout, whitefish, red snapper or pickerel), cleaned	1 kg
3 tbsp	soy sauce	50 mL
2 tbsp	dry sherry	25 mL
1 tbsp	fermented black beans, rinsed and chopped*	15 mL
1 tbsp	finely chopped gingerroot	15 mL
1 tsp	sesame oil	5 mL
2	green onions, julienned	2
1	small carrot, julienned (optional)	1

• Remove fish head; cut off tail if desired. Diagonally slash skin 3 times on each side. Place on microwaveable serving platter. Combine soy sauce, sherry, black beans, ginger and oil; spoon into fish cavity and over fish. Let marinate for 15 minutes.

• Sprinkle fish with onions; cover with vented plastic wrap. Microwave at High for 5 to 8 minutes or until fish is opaque and flakes easily when tested with fork close to backbone, rotating dish twice and basting with marinade halfway through. Sprinkle with carrot (if using). Makes 4 servings.

*Available at Chinese food stores.

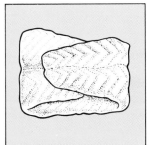

To avoid overcooking the thinner ends of fish fillets, fold both ends underneath the center of each fillet.

SOLE FILLETS WITH MUSHROOM-TOMATO CREAM SAUCE

A quick cream sauce makes sole fancy enough for guests.

1 lb	sole fillets	500 g
1 cup	sliced mushrooms	250 mL
1	tomato, peeled, seeded and chopped	1
2 tbsp	chopped green onion	25 mL
1/4 cup	dry white wine	50 mL
1/2 cup	whipping cream	125 mL
1 tbsp	cornstarch	15 mL
1 tsp	lemon juice	5 mL
Pinch	cayenne pepper	Pinch
	Salt and black pepper	
2 tbsp	chopped fresh parsley	25 mL

• Fold both ends of each fillet underneath center and arrange like spokes of a wheel in 10-inch (25 cm) pie plate. Sprinkle mushrooms, tomato and onion evenly over fish; drizzle with wine. Cover with vented plastic wrap; microwave at High for 3 to 5 minutes or until fish is opaque, rotating dish once. Drain off cooking juices and reserve. Let fish stand, covered, for 2 minutes.

• Meanwhile, in 2-cup (500 mL) measure, blend together cream and cornstarch; stir in reserved cooking liquid. Microwave at High for 1 to 1-1/2 minutes or until thickened, whisking once. Stir in lemon juice, cayenne, and salt and pepper to taste. Pour over fish; sprinkle with parsley. Makes 4 servings.

Oriental Whole Fish

WHOLE FISH WITH RICE STUFFING

Because a whole fish can be difficult to transfer after it has been cooked, you'll find it easier to cook it right on the serving platter.

2-1/4 lb	whole fish (salmon trout or whitefish)	625 g
1 tbsp	butter	15 mL
1/2 cup	sliced mushrooms	125 mL
1/4 cup	sliced green onions	50 mL
1 cup	cooked rice	250 mL
2 tbsp	chopped fresh parsley	25 mL
1/2 tsp	salt	2 mL
1/4 tsp	dried thyme (or 1/2 tsp/2 mL fresh)	1 mL
	Pepper	
1	lemon, cut in wedges	1

• Rinse fish under cold running water; remove head and tail. Pat dry inside and out. Set aside.
• In 4-cup (1 L) measure, microwave butter at High for 30 to 45 seconds or until melted. Stir in mushrooms and onions; microwave at High for 1 minute or just until softened. Add rice, parsley, salt, thyme, and pepper to taste; mix well. Stuff fish with rice mixture.
• Place on large microwaveable serving platter; cover with vented plastic wrap. Microwave at High for 7 to 11 minutes or until fish is opaque and flakes easily when tested with fork near backbone, rotating dish twice. Let stand for 5 minutes. Serve with lemon wedges. Makes 6 servings.

If your microwave oven will accomodate a whole fish, it can be baked with head and tail left on, if desired. To prevent overcooking, simply shield the head (especially the eye) and the thin tail end with pieces of aluminum foil. Remove the foil for the final 3 to 4 minutes at High.

SCALLOP AND FISH COQUILLES

These cheesy creamy coquilles are easy to make and elegant enough for guests.

1	pkg (7 oz/198 g) individually frozen scallops	1
1/2 lb	fish fillets	250 g
2 tbsp	butter	25 mL
2 tbsp	all-purpose flour	25 mL
3/4 cup	milk	175 mL
1 cup	shredded Cheddar cheese	250 mL
2 tbsp	dry vermouth or white wine	25 mL
	Salt and pepper	
2 tbsp	dry bread crumbs	25 mL

• In shallow microwaveable baking dish, arrange scallops in single layer; cover with waxed paper. Microwave at High for 5 minutes or until opaque, stirring once. Drain, reserving 1/3 cup (75 mL) cooking liquid; set aside.
• Pat fish fillets dry and cut into 1-inch (2.5 cm) pieces. In shallow dish, arrange in single layer; cover with waxed paper. Microwave at High for 2 minutes or until opaque; set aside.
• In 2-cup (500 mL) glass measure, microwave butter at High for 40 to 50 seconds or until melted; stir in flour until smooth. Stir in reserved cooking liquid and milk; microwave at High for 2-1/2 to 3 minutes or until sauce bubbles and thickens, stirring once. Mix in half of the cheese; stir in vermouth and scallops. Season with salt and pepper to taste.
• Divide fish among four scallop shells or 1-cup (250 mL) baking dishes. Top with scallop mixture. Sprinkle with remaining cheese and bread crumbs. Broil on baking sheet 6 inches (15 cm) from heat for 1-1/2 to 2 minutes or until bubbly and lightly browned. Makes 4 servings.

*Clams and Mussels with
Wine and Herbs*

CLAMS AND MUSSELS WITH WINE AND HERBS

*Each clam and mussel has its own cooking
time. Remove from cooking dish as each one
opens, to prevent overcooking.*

1 lb	clams	500 g
1 lb	mussels	500 g
2 tbsp	butter	25 mL
2	cloves garlic, minced	2
4	green onions, chopped	4
1/4 cup	dry white wine	50 mL
1/4 tsp	crushed black peppercorns	1 mL
2 tbsp	chopped fresh parsley	25 mL
2 tbsp	chopped fresh dill	25 mL

• Scrub clams and mussels under cold running
water; remove any beards from mussels.
Discard any mussels and clams that are not
tightly closed. Arrange clams around outside
edge of 9-inch (23 cm) pie plate or low casserole dish. Arrange mussels around outside
edge of a similar dish. Set seafood aside.

• In 2-cup (500 mL) measure, combine
butter, garlic and green onions; microwave
at High, uncovered, for 2 minutes or until
onions are softened. Stir in wine and
peppercorns; microwave at High for 1 minute
or until mixture comes to boil.

• Pour half of the wine mixture over clams.
Cover with vented plastic wrap; microwave at
High for 2-1/2 to 5 minutes or until clams
open, removing clams as they open and
rotating dish once. Discard any that do not
open. Drain off and reserve juices; cover
clams and let stand for 2 minutes.

• Pour remaining wine mixture over mussels.
Cover with vented plastic wrap; microwave
at High for 2 to 4 minutes or until mussels
open, removing mussels as they open and
rotating dish once. Discard any that do not
open. Drain off juices; add to clam juices.
Cover mussels and let stand for 2 minutes.

• Meanwhile, microwave reserved seafood
juices at High for 2 minutes. Arrange seafood
in bowl and spoon juices evenly over top.
Sprinkle with parsley and dill. Makes 2 main-
course servings or 4 appetizers.

MEDITERRANEAN FISH STEW

Team this flavorful stew with French bread and a fruit salad for a complete meal.

1 tbsp	olive oil	15 mL
2	cloves garlic, minced	2
1	onion, chopped	1
1	leek (white part), sliced	1
1 tbsp	tomato paste	15 mL
2	tomatoes, peeled, seeded and chopped	2
4 cups	chicken stock	1 L
1/2 cup	dry white wine	125 mL
	Bouquet garni*	
Pinch	saffron	Pinch
1 lb	monkfish	500 g
1 lb	cod or haddock	500 g
3/4 lb	mussels, cleaned and beards removed	375 g
	Salt and pepper	
	Croutes (recipe follows)	
	Rouille (recipe follows)	
2 tbsp	chopped fresh parsley	25 mL
	Strips orange rind (optional)	

• In 12-cup (3 L) casserole, combine, oil, garlic, onion and leek; microwave at High for 3 to 4 minutes or until onion and leek are softened. Stir in tomato paste. Add tomatoes, stock, wine, bouquet garni and saffron; mix well. Cover with lid or vented plastic wrap and microwave at High for 10 minutes. Meanwhile, cut monkfish and cod into 2-inch (5 cm) chunks; add to soup and microwave at High for 2 to 6 minutes or until fish is opaque, rotating dish once.

• Arrange mussels, hinges toward center, around outside edge of large round shallow dish. Cover with vented plastic wrap and microwave at High for 2 to 4 minutes or until shells open, rotating dish once. Discard any that do not open. Drain, stirring juices into soup. Season soup with salt and pepper to taste.

• Spread each croute with some rouille; place one on bottom of each warmed soup bowl. Ladle soup into bowls and arrange mussels on top. Sprinkle with parsley. Garnish with orange rind (if using). Pass remaining rouille separately to stir into soup if desired. Makes 6 main-course servings.

*Bouquet garni: In double thickness of cheesecloth, tie together 1/2 tsp (2 mL) fennel seeds, pinch thyme, 3 sprigs parsley, 1 bay leaf and strip of orange rind.

ALTERNATE SERVING SUGGESTIONS
• *Serve Mediterranean Fish Stew without Croutes and swirl Rouille on top of each serving for a tasty and decorative effect.*
• *Instead of Rouille, spread Parsley Pesto, Basil Pesto or Coriander Pesto (recipes, p. 53) on the Croutes. Ladle the stew over top and garnish with the corresponding fresh herbs.*

CROUTES:

6	thick slices French stick (baguette)	6

• On plate, arrange bread slices in circle; microwave at High for 2 to 4 minutes or until dry and firm, rotating plate once.

ROUILLE:

1	jar (4-1/2 oz/ 128 mL) sliced pimiento, drained	1
3	cloves garlic, minced	3
2 tbsp	olive oil	25 mL
Dash	hot pepper sauce	Dash
2 tbsp	bread crumbs	25 mL
	Salt	

• In food processor or blender, purée pimiento and garlic until smooth. Blend in oil and hot pepper sauce. Stir in bread crumbs until well blended. Season with salt to taste.

Mediterranean Fish Stew

SPICY SHRIMP

The subtle warmth of this pleasantly spiced dish is very appealing. Serve over rice or noodles.

1	small onion, chopped	1
1	small sweet green pepper, slivered	1
1/2 cup	sliced celery	125 mL
1	clove garlic, minced	1
2 tbsp	butter	25 mL
2 tbsp	all-purpose flour	25 mL
1	can (14 oz/398 mL) tomatoes (undrained)	1
1	can (7-1/2 oz/ 213 mL) tomato sauce	1
1 tsp	chili powder	5 mL
Dash	hot pepper sauce	Dash
3/4 lb	shrimp, peeled and deveined	375 g
	Salt and pepper	
2 tbsp	chopped fresh parsley	25 mL

• In 8-cup (2 L) dish, combine onion, green pepper, celery, garlic and butter; microwave at High, uncovered, for 3 to 4 minutes or until vegetables are tender-crisp, stirring partway through.
• Add flour and stir until well blended. Stir in tomatoes, tomato sauce, chili powder and hot pepper sauce; cover and microwave at High for 10 minutes or until thickened and bubbling, stirring twice.
• Add shrimp; stir to mix. Cover and microwave at High for 3 to 5 minutes or until shrimp are bright pink and opaque, stirring once. Season with salt and pepper to taste. Let stand for 5 minutes. Garnish with parsley. Makes about 4 servings.

Eggs and Cheese

Scrambled eggs are a breeze in the microwave – and there's no messy pan left to scrub afterwards. Dress scrambled eggs up with smoked salmon (p. 110) or mound them in a spinach ring (p. 18) and you have the centerpiece for a stylish brunch. Try the Italian-style Ham and Spinach Frittata (p. 112) that pairs eggs with creamy ricotta cheese. Even classic Eggs Benedict (p. 108) becomes easier when you make the hollandaise sauce (p. 158) with the help of your microwave. Another traditional favorite, Cheese Fondue (p. 115), makes a great treat for après-ski.

POACHED EGGS WITH SALSA MEXICANA

For a Mexican-style lunch or brunch, combine this colorful egg dish with piping hot Spicy Sausage Patties (recipe, p. 65). This method is a good way to poach eggs individually.

1/2 cup	water	125 mL
1 tsp	vinegar	5 mL
4	eggs	4
	Salsa Mexicana (recipe follows)	

• Stir together water and vinegar; place about 2 tbsp (25 mL) in each of four 3/4-cup (175 mL) custard cups. Microwave at High for 1 to 2 minutes or until boiling. Break 1 egg into each cup; puncture yolks lightly with skewer. Cover with vented plastic wrap and arrange in oven in circle with 1-inch (2.5 cm) space between cups. Microwave at Medium (50%) for 2-1/2 to 3 minutes or until eggs are nearly set, rotating dishes once. Let stand for about 2 minutes or until set. Remove from cups to serving plates. Serve with Salsa Mexicana. Makes 4 servings.

SALSA MEXICANA:

1	small onion, finely chopped	1
1	clove garlic, minced	1
1 tbsp	vegetable oil	15 mL
1 cup	chopped drained canned tomatoes	250 mL
1/4 tsp	hot pepper flakes	1 mL
1 tbsp	finely chopped fresh coriander or parsley	15 mL
	Salt	

• In small bowl, combine onion, garlic and oil; microwave at High for 2 minutes or until onion is softened. Stir in tomatoes and hot pepper flakes; microwave at High for 3 to 4 minutes or until heated through and flavors are blended. Stir in coriander; season with salt to taste. Serve hot or cold. Makes 1 cup (250 mL).

Poached Eggs with Salsa Mexicana; Spicy Sausage Patties (p. 65)

BAKED EGGS IN MUSHROOM SAUCE

Served with toasted whole-wheat English muffins and tossed greens, baked eggs are great for brunch or a light supper.

1 tbsp	butter	15 mL
1/3 cup	chopped green onions or chives	75 mL
1/2 tsp	curry powder	2 mL
1/2 lb	mushrooms, chopped (about 2-1/4 cups/550 mL)	250 g
1 tbsp	all-purpose flour	15 mL
1/2 cup	light cream or milk	125 mL
1/2 tsp	salt	2 mL
	Pepper	
4	eggs	4
1/4 cup	shredded Cheddar cheese	50 mL

• In 8-cup (2 L) measure, microwave butter at High for 20 seconds or until melted. Add onions and curry powder; microwave at High for about 1 minute or until onions are softened. Add mushrooms; microwave at High for 2 to 4 minutes or until softened, stirring halfway through. Stir in flour until well blended. Stir in cream, salt, and pepper to taste; microwave at High for 2 to 4 minutes or until sauce has thickened, stirring halfway through.
• Evenly divide mushroom sauce between 2 lightly greased 1-1/2-cup (375 mL) baking dishes. Carefully drop 2 eggs into each dish, using spoon to push sauce up side of dish to form nest. Pierce yolks gently; cover loosely with waxed paper. Microwave at High for 1 minute; microwave at Medium-High (70%) for 4 to 6 minutes or until whites are set but yolks are still soft, turning dishes once.
• Sprinkle evenly with cheese; microwave, uncovered, at Medium-High (70%) for 30 seconds or until cheese has melted. Let stand for 1 minute. Makes 2 servings.

EGGS BENEDICT

Did you ever dream Eggs Benedict could be so easy to prepare? This version with Microwave Blender Hollandaise (recipe, p. 158) can be ready in minutes.

	Microwave Blender Hollandaise(recipe, p. 158)	
2	English muffins	2
	Butter	
4	slices Black Forest ham	4
4	poached eggs (sidebar, this page)	4

• Split English muffins and toast halves; lightly spread with butter.
• Place ham on paper towel-lined plate; cover with vented plastic wrap and microwave at High for 1 minute or just until warm.
• Place 1 slice ham on each muffin half; top with poached egg. Spoon warm Hollandaise over eggs. Makes 4 servings.

POACHED EGGS
• *Break egg into small bowl. Carefully pierce egg yolk with toothpick. In 2-cup (500 mL) measure, combine 1 cup (250 mL) water and 1/2 tsp (2 mL) vinegar; microwave at High for 2 to 3 minutes or until boiling. Stir water to swirl; slip in egg. Cover with vented plastic wrap and microwave at Medium-High (70%) for 40 to 60 seconds or until almost set. Let stand, covered, for 1 minute. For 2 eggs, use 4-cup (1 L) measure, 1-1/2 cups (375 mL) water and 3/4 tsp (5 mL) vinegar; microwave for 1 to 1-1/2 minutes.*

Eggs and Ham Creole

EGGS AND HAM CREOLE

When you want to create a delicious and different breakfast or lunch, try this hearty Western-style method of cooking ham and eggs.

2 tbsp	butter	25 mL
1	clove garlic, minced	1
1	small onion, finely chopped	1
1	small sweet green pepper, diced	1
1	stalk celery, diced	1
1	tomato, diced	1
1	can (7-1/2 oz/ 213 mL) tomato sauce	1
1/2 tsp	dried thyme	2 mL
1/4 tsp	hot pepper sauce	1 mL
	Salt and pepper	
1/2 lb	Black Forest ham, diced	250 g
4	eggs	4
3/4 cup	shredded Monterey Jack or mild Cheddar cheese	175 mL

• In 8-cup (2 L) measure, combine butter, garlic, onion, green pepper and celery; microwave at High for 4 to 6 minutes or until softened, stirring halfway through.
• Add tomato, tomato sauce, thyme, hot pepper sauce, and salt and pepper to taste. Microwave at High for 4 to 5 minutes or until hot and bubbly. Stir in ham.
• Divide mixture among 4 lightly buttered 1-cup (250 mL) gratin or baking dishes. With spoon, make a hollow in each tomato mixture; break eggs into hollows. Gently pierce yolks.
• Cover loosely with waxed paper; microwave at High for 1 minute. Microwave at Medium-High (70%) for 5 to 7 minutes or until whites are set but yolks are still soft, turning dishes if necessary.
• Sprinkle with cheese. Microwave at Medium-High (70%), uncovered, for 1 to 2 minutes or until cheese has melted. Let stand for 2 to 3 minutes before serving. Makes 4 servings.

Scrambled Eggs with Smoked Salmon; Sliced Tomatoes Parmesan (p. 34)

SCRAMBLED EGGS WITH SMOKED SALMON

Here is a breakfast to serve in style. Your prettiest tablecloth, best china and a vase of fresh flowers will provide the proper setting for this aristocratic dish.

1 tbsp	butter	15 mL
6	eggs	6
3 tbsp	milk	50 mL
Pinch	white pepper	Pinch
1/2 cup	chopped smoked salmon	125 mL
1/4 cup	chopped green onion	50 mL
2 tbsp	sour cream	25 mL
1 tbsp	chopped fresh coriander or parsley	15 mL

• In 6-cup (1.5 L) bowl, microwave butter at High for 20 to 40 seconds or until melted. With wire whisk or fork, beat in eggs, milk and pepper until well blended. Microwave at High, uncovered, for 2 to 3 minutes or until some curds have formed but mixture is still creamy, stirring twice.
• Stir in salmon, green onion, sour cream and coriander. Microwave at High for 30 to 60 seconds or until eggs are heated through and still creamy, stirring once. Makes 3 or 4 servings.

GENERAL TIPS
• *Never microwave a whole egg in its shell.*
• *Since microwaves are attracted to fat in egg yolks, the yolk cooks as fast or faster than the white. Scrambled eggs, where yolk and white are well mixed and stirred several times, can be cooked at a higher power level than an omelette that is not stirred.*
• *Pierce egg yolk gently 2 or 3 times before poaching or frying. This keeps pressure from building up inside the membrane that surrounds the yolk and prevents possible bursting.*
• *Always undercook eggs slightly and allow a short standing time before serving or chilling.*

MICROWAVE YOUR FAVORITE EGGS

• *Steam-Poached:* This method is simpler than the classic method described on page 108. Break 1 egg into buttered custard cup. Using toothpick, pierce yolk; cover with vented plastic wrap. Microwave at Medium-High (70%) for 45 to 60 seconds for 1 egg, 1 to 1-1/2 minutes for 2 eggs, 1-1/2 to 2 minutes for 3 eggs or until just set. Let stand for 1 to 2 minutes.

• *Hard-Cooked:* Eggs hard-cooked in the microwave oven will not look the same as stove-top hard-cooked, but they are fine for sandwich fillings or recipes calling for chopped hard-cooked eggs. Follow the same steps as for steam-poaching, but continue cooking until yolks are firm. Let stand for 5 minutes; chill.

• *Frying:* To fry 1 or 2 eggs in the microwave, preheat browning dish at High for 2 minutes, or according to manufacturer's directions. Meanwhile, break each egg into saucer or custard cup; prick yolks. Add 1 tsp (5 mL) butter to heated browning dish while still in oven, spreading quickly over surface. Gently add eggs. Microwave, uncovered, at Medium-High (70%) for about 1-1/2 minutes or until eggs are set to desired doneness. Cover and let stand for 2 minutes.

PUFFY OMELETTE

Make this easy dish with any of the suggested fillings, or mix and match them to your taste. If using green onion, microwave it with 2 tsp (10 mL) butter at High for 1 minute before adding to the omelette.

2 tsp	butter	10 mL
3	eggs, separated	3
1 tbsp	water	15 mL
	Salt and pepper	

FILLING SUGGESTIONS:

1/2 cup	shredded cheese (preferably orange Cheddar)	125 mL
1/4 cup	crumbled cooked bacon	50 mL
1	tomato, seeded and chopped	1
2 tbsp	cooked chopped green onion	25 mL
2 tsp	chopped fresh herbs (basil, thyme, oregano or chives)	10 mL

• In 9-inch (23 cm) pie plate, microwave butter at High for 30 seconds or until melted; swirl to coat bottom and sides of plate.
• In bowl, beat egg whites until stiff and glossy. Whisk together egg yolks, water, and salt and pepper to taste; fold into whites. Pour into pie plate and spread smoothly.
• Microwave, uncovered, at Medium-High (70%) for 1-1/2 minutes, rotating once. Microwave at High for 30 to 60 seconds or until center is barely set.
• **Filling:** Make slit down center of omelette; spoon in filling of your choice. Fold omelette over and slide onto plate. Makes 2 or 3 servings.

HANDY CHART FOR SCRAMBLING EGGS

Eggs	Butter	Milk or Water	Cooking Time
1	1/2 tsp (2 mL)	1 tbsp (15 mL)	35 to 40 seconds
2	1 tsp (5 mL)	2 tbsp (25 mL)	1 to 1-1/2 minutes
4	2 tsp (10 mL)	1/4 cup (50 mL)	2 to 2-1/2 minutes
6	1 tbsp (15 mL)	1/3 cup (75 mL)	3 to 3-1/2 minutes

• *Scrambled eggs puff and rise, so cook in the container specified.*
• *In small bowl for 1 or 2 eggs, medium bowl for 4 to 6 eggs, microwave butter at High for 10 to 20 seconds or until melted. Using fork, blend in eggs and milk. Microwave, uncovered, at High until eggs begin to set but still look moist and creamy, whisking every 30 seconds.*

SEASONAL FRITTATA

Vary the flavor of this dish by taking advantage of fresh seasonal fruit such as peaches, plums or apples.

1 tbsp	butter	15 mL
1 tbsp	vegetable oil	15 mL
2	green onions, sliced	2
1	small sweet green pepper, chopped	1
1	pear (preferably small Bartlett or Bosc), peeled, cored and sliced	1
4	eggs	4
1/4 lb	Swiss cheese, shredded (about 1 cup/250 mL)	125 g
1/2 cup	fresh whole wheat bread crumbs	125 mL
Dash	hot pepper sauce	Dash
	Salt and pepper	

• In large bowl, combine butter, oil, onions, green pepper and pear. Cover with vented plastic wrap and microwave at High for 2 minutes. Beat eggs until frothy; add to bowl along with cheese, bread crumbs, hot pepper sauce, and salt and pepper to taste.
• Divide mixture among 4 buttered 1-cup (250 mL) microwaveable serving dishes; cover with vented plastic wrap. Microwave at Medium-High (70%) for about 6 minutes or until almost set in centers, rotating twice. Let stand for 5 minutes. Makes 4 servings.

HAM AND SPINACH FRITTATA

Here's a classic Italian egg dish that makes a wonderful main course served with crusty rolls and a green salad.

4 cups	loosely packed spinach	1 L
1	onion, sliced	1
2 tsp	butter	10 mL
5	eggs	5
1 cup	smooth ricotta cheese	250 mL
1 tsp	dried basil	5 mL
1/2 tsp	salt	2 mL
Pinch	pepper	Pinch
1/2 cup	freshly grated Parmesan cheese	125 mL
1/4 lb	Black Forest ham, chopped	125 g

• Rinse spinach; place in 12-cup (3 L) casserole with just the water clinging to leaves. Cover with lid or vented plastic wrap and microwave at High for 5 to 6 minutes or just until wilted, stirring once. Drain and rinse under cold running water. Squeeze out excess moisture, chop coarsely and set aside.
• In small bowl, microwave onion and butter at High for 1 to 2 minutes or until onion is softened. Set aside.
• In food processor, combine eggs, ricotta cheese, basil, salt and pepper; process until smooth. Transfer to bowl; stir in Parmesan, ham, reserved spinach and onion mixture. Pour into greased 9- or 10-inch (23 or 25 cm) quiche dish or pie plate; microwave, uncovered, at Medium (50%) for 12 to 15 minutes or until almost set in center, rotating twice. Let stand for 5 minutes. Makes 4 to 6 servings.

Ham and Spinach Frittata; Beet, Endive and Watercress Salad (p. 131)

BACON AND TOMATO QUICHE

Bacon and Tomato Quiche

A tossed salad and crusty bread completes this fast and easy supper.

6	slices bacon	6
1 tbsp	butter, softened	15 mL
1/2 cup	bread crumbs	125 mL
2	tomatoes, sliced and well drained	2
1 cup	shredded Cheddar cheese	250 mL
1/2 tsp	dried oregano	2 mL
1/4 tsp	celery seed	1 mL
1/4 tsp	dried thyme	1 mL
	Pepper	
1 cup	milk	250 mL
4	eggs	4

• Between paper towels, microwave bacon at High for 4 to 6 minutes or just until cooked, rotating halfway through. Let stand to cool.

• Brush 9-inch (23 cm) pie plate with butter; sprinkle with 1/4 cup (50 mL) of the bread crumbs. Arrange half of the tomatoes in single layer over crumbs; sprinkle with half of the cheese, 1/4 tsp (1 mL) of the oregano, celery seed, thyme, and pepper to taste. Repeat layering with remaining tomatoes, cheese and bread crumbs; sprinkle with remaining oregano, and pepper to taste. Crumble bacon over top; set aside.

• Microwave milk at High for 1-1/2 to 2 minutes or until steaming. In bowl, lightly whisk eggs; slowly whisk in hot milk. Pour over quiche. Microwave, uncovered, at Medium (50%) for 8 to 10 minutes or just until center is almost set, rotating every 2 minutes. Let stand for 10 minutes or until firm in center and knife inserted comes out clean. Makes 4 to 6 servings.

OVERNIGHT STRATAS

Make these individual stratas the night before and pop each one into the microwave when you're ready to eat in the morning.

2	slices whole wheat or multi-grain bread	2
1-1/2 cups	shredded Swiss cheese	375 mL
2 tsp	chopped fresh parsley	10 mL
2	eggs	2
1 cup	milk	250 mL
1/2 tsp	salt	2 mL
1/4 tsp	dry mustard	1 mL
Dash	hot pepper sauce (optional)	Dash
	Pepper	

• Cube bread; toss with cheese and parsley. Divide between two greased 2-cup (500 mL) baking dishes.
• Lightly whisk together eggs, milk, salt, mustard, hot pepper sauce (if using), and pepper to taste. Pour half of the egg mixture into each dish, filling no more than two-thirds full. Cover and refrigerate overnight.
• Cover with vented plastic wrap; microwave, one at a time, at Medium (50%) for about 6 minutes or until set, rotating dish twice. Let stand for 2 minutes. Makes 2 servings.

CHEESE FONDUE

Ideal for company, this classic Swiss fondue will have a better balance of flavor if you use equal amounts of Gruyère and Emmenthal cheese.

1	clove garlic, halved	1
4 cups	shredded Swiss cheese (about 1 lb/ 500 g)	1 L
1/4 cup	all-purpose flour	50 mL
Pinch	each cayenne pepper and nutmeg	Pinch
1 cup	dry white wine	250 mL
2 tbsp	kirsch (optional)	25 mL
	Salt and pepper	
	Bread cubes	

• Rub 6-cup (1.5 L) casserole with cut garlic and discard. Combine cheese, flour, cayenne pepper and nutmeg; toss well and set aside.
• Pour wine into casserole; microwave, uncovered, at High for 1 to 3 minutes or just until bubbles begin to form but wine does not boil. Stir in cheese mixture; microwave, uncovered, at Medium (50%) for 4 to 8 minutes or until melted and well blended, stirring every 2 minutes.
• Stir in kirsch (if using); season with salt and pepper to taste. Serve with bread cubes. Makes 4 to 5 servings.

• *Cheese needs a low power level for cooking. Overcooking causes the cheese to toughen and the fat to separate out.*
• *Cooking time depends on the temperature of the cheese at the start of cooking (room temperature or from the refrigerator) and the form (cubes, slices or shredded).*
• *To prevent a cheese topping from becoming stringy, sprinkle shredded cheese over casserole after cooking. Cover with foil, shiny side down; let cheese melt during standing time.*

Pasta, Rice and Grains

While the pasta cooks on your stove top, you can prepare marvelous sauces in the microwave and then combine them for an appetizing main dish. Try Linguine with Eggplant and Tomato Sauce (p. 123) or Vermicelli with Broccoli Pesto Sauce (p. 118) – serve with a green salad and dinner's on the table! Lemon Rice (p. 122) or Barley Pilaf (p. 122) makes a pleasant change from potatoes and if you've ever stirred risotto for twenty minutes, you'll love the almost effortless Risotto with Peas (p. 116).

RISOTTO WITH PEAS

Risotto is a dish many chefs shy away from because it needs constant stirring. But this microwave version of the Italian classic is almost effortless. Arborio, Italian short-grain rice, is what gives risotto its characteristic nutty flavor and creamy texture.

1-3/4 cups	chicken stock	425 mL
2 tbsp	butter	25 mL
1	onion, chopped	1
3/4 cup	short-grain rice	175 mL
1/2 cup	frozen peas	125 mL
1/3 cup	grated Parmesan cheese	75 mL
	Salt and pepper	

• In 4-cup (1 L) measure, microwave stock at High for 3 to 4 minutes or until simmering. Set aside.

• In 12-cup (3 L) deep casserole, combine butter and onion. Microwave at High for 2 minutes, or until onion has softened, stirring once. Add rice; stir to coat rice with butter. Pour in hot stock; cover with lid or vented plastic wrap and microwave at High for 4 to 5 minutes or until boiling. Microwave at Medium (50%) for 7 to 9 minutes, or until rice is just tender and mixture is still creamy, rotating once if necessary. Rinse peas with warm water to thaw and stir into rice mixture. Cover and let stand 5 minutes. Stir in cheese. Taste and adjust seasoning with salt and pepper. Makes 4 servings.

MICRO-STEAMED RICE

Type of Rice	Amount	Water	Salt	Cooking Time	Standing Time
Long Grain Rice Short Grain Rice Parboiled Rice	1 cup (250 mL)	2 cups (500 mL)	1/2 tsp (2 mL)	High: 4 to 7 min Medium (50%): 10 to 12 minutes	10 minutes
Brown Rice	1 cup (250 mL)	2 1/2 cups (625 mL)	1/2 tsp (2 mL)	High: 4 to 7 min Medium (50%): 25 to 35 minutes	10 minutes

• In 12-cup (3 L) casserole, combine water, rice and salt. Cover with lid or vented plastic wrap and microwave at High for 4 to 7 minutes or until water begins to boil. Microwave at Medium (50%) for times given in chart or until most of the liquid is absorbed and rice is tender, rotating dish twice. Let stand, covered, for 10 minutes. Makes 4 servings.

Risotto with Peas

VERMICELLI WITH BROCCOLI PESTO SAUCE

Vermicelli with Broccoli Pesto Sauce

Treat yourself to a taste of early summer with this broccoli pesto sauce served over vermicelli noodles.

3 tbsp	pine nuts	50 mL
1/3 cup	olive oil	75 mL
4 cups	broccoli florets	1 L
1	clove garlic	1
1/4 cup	fresh parsley	50 mL
1 tbsp	fresh basil (or 1 tsp/5 mL dry)	15 mL
1/4 cup	freshly grated Parmesan cheese	50 mL
	Salt and pepper	
1/2 lb	vermicelli or capelli d'angelo	

• On glass pie plate, mix pine nuts with 1 tsp (5 mL) of the olive oil; cover with waxed paper and microwave at High for 3 to 4 minutes or until lightly browned, stirring two or three times. Set aside.

• In large bowl, cover broccoli with vented plastic wrap and microwave at High for 4 minutes or just until tender.

• Meanwhile, in blender or food processor, combine garlic, parsley, basil and 2 tbsp (25 mL) of the toasted pine nuts; process until very finely chopped.

• Drain broccoli, reserving a few florets for garnish. Add remainder to blender along with remaining oil and Parmesan cheese; process until well blended but slightly coarse, scraping down sides of container as necessary. Season with salt and pepper to taste. Set aside.

• In large pot of boiling salted water, cook pasta according to package directions or until al dente (tender but firm). Drain and toss with broccoli pesto. Serve garnished with remaining pine nuts and reserved broccoli florets. Makes about 4 servings.

For perfect timing of pasta dishes, cook the pasta on top of your stove (according to package directions) while making the sauce in the microwave oven.

SEAFOOD LASAGNA

This is a great make-ahead dish. Cook the lasagna noodles conventionally on the stove top for the best texture or use precooked lasagna noodles. If you're using frozen seafood, make sure it's thawed and thoroughly drained beforehand.

9	lasagna noodles	9
TOMATO SEAFOOD SAUCE:		
1/3 cup	finely chopped onion	75 mL
1	clove garlic, minced	1
2 tsp	olive oil	10 mL
Pinch	hot pepper flakes	Pinch
1-1/2 cups	crushed tomatoes	375 mL
1/4 cup	chopped fresh basil (or 2 tsp/10 mL dried)	50 mL
2 tbsp	white wine	25 mL
1/2 lb	crab meat	250 g
1/2 lb	chopped poached shrimp*	250 g
3 tbsp	whipping cream	50 mL
CHEESE FILLING:		
1-1/2 cups	packed spinach	375 mL
1 cup	ricotta cheese	250 mL
1	egg, beaten	1
1/2 lb	poached halved scallops**	250 g
2 tbsp	chopped green onion	25 mL
2 tbsp	chopped fresh parsley	25 mL
	Salt and pepper	
1-1/2 cups	shredded mozzarella cheese	375 mL

You can use the Tomato Seafood Sauce and the Cheese Filling for more than just Lasagna.
- *Tomato Seafood Sauce is delicious over cooked rice or noodles and can turn simple microwaved fish fillets into company fare.*
- *Cheese Filling can be used to fill jumbo pasta shells, cannelloni or manicotti and served with a light tomato sauce.*

- In large pot of boiling water, cook pasta until al dente (tender but firm); drain and set aside.
- **Tomato Seafood Sauce:** In large bowl, combine onion, garlic, olive oil and hot pepper flakes. Microwave at High for 2 to 2-1/2 minutes or until softened, stirring once. Add tomatoes, basil and wine. Microwave at High for 3 minutes, stirring once. Mix in crab meat, shrimp and cream. Set aside.
- **Cheese Filling:** In bowl, cover spinach with vented plastic wrap and microwave at High for 1 minute; drain well and chop. Return to bowl. Stir in ricotta cheese and egg. Fold in scallops, onion and parsley. Season with salt and pepper to taste. Set aside.
- **Assembly:** In greased 11- x 7-inch (2 L) casserole, spread thin layer of tomato sauce; top with 3 lasagna noodles, trimming to fit if necessary. Cover with half of the remaining tomato sauce. Sprinkle with half of the mozzarella cheese and cover with 3 lasagna noodles. Spread cheese filling evenly over noodles. Finish with last 3 noodles, then top with remaining tomato sauce. Cover lasagna with plastic wrap and refrigerate for up to 1 day.
- Turn back one corner of plastic wrap and microwave at High for 5 minutes. Rotate dish and microwave at Medium (50%) for 8 to 14 minutes or until hot in center, rotating once. If serving lasagna without refrigerating, microwave at High for 5 minutes. Rotate dish and microwave at Medium (50%) for 5 to 8 minutes or until heated through.
- Remove plastic wrap; sprinkle lasagna with remaining mozzarella. Cover with foil, shiny side down; let stand for 10 minutes to melt cheese. Makes 6 servings.

*To poach shrimp: Peel and devein shrimp. In small bowl, microwave 1 cup (250 mL) water at High for 2 to 2-1/2 minutes or until boiling. Add thick lemon slice and shrimp. Microwave at High for 1 to 1-1/2 minutes or until shrimp turn pink, stirring once. Drain.

**To poach scallops: Halve scallops. In small bowl, microwave 1 cup (250 mL) water at High for 2 to 2-1/2 minutes or until boiling. Add lemon slice and scallops. Microwave at High for 30 to 45 seconds or until opaque, stirring once. Drain.

DELUXE MACARONI AND CHEESE

Ordinary macaroni and cheese becomes a special dish when it's layered with cheese as well as bathed in a cheesy sauce.

6 cups	drained cooked elbow macaroni	1.5 L
2 cups	Cheese Sauce (recipe, p. 159)	500 mL
1-1/2 cups	shredded Cheddar cheese	375 mL
2 tbsp	dry bread crumbs	25 mL
1 tbsp	chopped fresh parsley	15 mL
2 tsp	butter, melted	10 mL

• Mix together macaroni and Cheese Sauce. In 12-cup (3 L) casserole, layer macaroni mixture with Cheddar cheese, making 3 layers, ending with cheese on top.
• Combine bread crumbs, parsley and butter; sprinkle over macaroni mixture. Cover with waxed paper and microwave at Medium (50%) for 10 to 12 minutes or until heated through, rotating dish twice. Makes 4 to 6 servings.

CANNELLONI

A delectable filling and appetizing sauce make this pasta dish extra-special. To make preparation easier, precooked cannelloni noodles can be purchased at many grocery stores.

12	precooked cannelloni noodles	12
FILLING:		
2 cups	packed spinach, stems removed	500 mL
1/2 lb	ricotta cheese	250 g
1/3 cup	freshly grated Parmesan cheese	75 mL
1/4 lb	diced ham	125 g
1	egg, lightly beaten	1
1/4 tsp	dried basil	1 mL
	Salt and pepper	
SAUCE:		
2 tbsp	olive oil	25 mL
1	clove garlic, minced	1
1	onion, finely chopped	1
1	can (19 oz/540 mL) tomatoes	1
1/4 cup	tomato paste	50 mL
1 tsp	dried basil	5 mL
1/2 tsp	dried oregano	2 mL
	Salt and pepper	

• **Filling:** Wash spinach; place in 8-cup (2 L) measure with just the water clinging to leaves. Cover with vented plastic wrap and microwave at High for 1 to 2 minutes or just until wilted. Drain and squeeze dry; finely chop.
• In large bowl, combine spinach, ricotta, 1/4 cup (50 mL) of the Parmesan, ham, egg, basil, and salt and pepper to taste; mix well and set aside.
• **Sauce:** In 8-cup (2 L) measure, combine oil, garlic and onion; microwave at High for 2 to 3 minutes or until softened. Add tomatoes, tomato paste, basil, oregano, and salt and pepper to taste; cover with waxed paper and microwave at High for 3 to 4 minutes or until heated through and slightly thickened, stirring halfway through.
• **Assembly:** Meanwhile, stuff noodles with filling. Spread 3/4 cup (175 mL) of the sauce in 8-inch (2 L) square or oval baking dish; arrange stuffed noodles in single layer over sauce and top with remaining sauce. Cover with waxed paper and microwave at High for 7 to 9 minutes or until heated through, rotating dish once.
• Sprinkle with remaining Parmesan. Let stand for 5 minutes before serving. Makes 4 servings.

Cannelloni

LEMON RICE

Lemon juice and rind add a refreshing flavor twist to plain rice.

2-1/4 cups	chicken stock	550 mL
1 cup	long-grain rice	250 mL
1 tbsp	butter	15 mL
1/2 tsp	salt	2 mL
1/4 cup	finely chopped fresh parsley	50 mL
1 tsp	finely grated lemon rind	5 mL
1 tbsp	lemon juice	15 mL

• In 10-cup (2.5 L) casserole, cover and microwave chicken stock, covered with lid or vented plastic wrap, at High for 4 to 5 minutes or until boiling.
• Stir in rice, butter and salt; cover and microwave at High for 5 minutes. Microwave, covered, at Medium-High (70%) for 10 minutes, rotating dish twice.
• Stir in parsley, lemon rind and juice. Let stand, covered, for 10 to 15 minutes or until all liquid has been absorbed. Fluff with fork. Makes 4 servings.

BARLEY PILAF

Potatoes or rice are the usual accompaniments for fish but this pilaf-style barley makes a nice change. You can make this dish first, then let stand while the fish cooks. If reheating is necessary, microwave at High for 2 minutes. Equally delicious with meat and poultry, the recipe can easily be doubled. Just increase the cooking time by about 4 minutes.

1/2 cup	sliced mushrooms	125 mL
2 tbsp	chopped onion	25 mL
1 tsp	butter	5 mL
1 cup	chicken stock	250 mL
1/2 cup	pearl barley	125 mL
1/4 cup	chopped chives	50 mL
	Salt and pepper	

• In 4-cup (1 L) glass measure, combine mushrooms, onion and butter; cover with vented plastic wrap and microwave at High for 1 minute. Add chicken stock and barley; microwave at High for 6 to 8 minutes or until barley is almost tender and most of the liquid is absorbed, stirring once. Add chives; cover and let stand for 10 minutes. Season with salt and pepper to taste. Makes 2 servings.

WILD RICE
To make 1 cup (250 mL) cooked wild rice: In a 4-cup (1 L) container, combine 1/2 cup (125 mL) wild rice with 1 cup (250 mL) chicken stock; microwave at High, covered with lid or vented plastic wrap, for about 3 minutes or until mixture comes to a boil. Let stand for 1 hour. Microwave, covered, at High for 10 minutes, stirring once; let stand for 5 minutes. Fluff with fork.

ALMOND RICE PILAF

For a gourmet touch, toast almonds in the microwave until golden. This pilaf is an ideal accompaniment for Salmon Ring with Hot Mayonnaise Sauce (recipe, p. 98).

1/3 cup	sliced almonds	75 mL
1 tsp	vegetable oil	5 mL
2 cups	water	500 mL
1 tbsp	butter	15 mL
1 cup	long-grain rice	250 mL
1 cup	frozen peas, thawed	250 mL

• In 9-inch (23 cm) pie plate, stir together almonds and oil until almonds are well coated. Microwave at High for 5 to 7 minutes or until light golden, stirring frequently and watching closely to prevent burning.
• In 8-cup (2 L) measure, combine water, butter and 1/2 tsp (2 mL) salt; microwave at High for 5 to 7 minutes or until boiling. Stir in rice; cover with vented plastic wrap; microwave at Medium-Low (30%) for 20 to 30 minutes or until water is absorbed and rice is tender. Toss peas with rice; cover and let stand for 5 minutes. Sprinkle with almonds. Makes 4 servings.

Linguine with Eggplant
and Tomato Sauce

LINGUINE WITH EGGPLANT AND TOMATO SAUCE

*Use your microwave to make the sauce while
you cook the pasta on top of the stove. Toss
together for a delicious meatless meal.*

1	medium eggplant	1
2	onions, sliced	2
1	sweet red pepper, sliced	1
1	clove garlic, minced	1
2 tbsp	olive oil	25 mL
1	can (28 oz/798 mL) plum tomatoes	1
1/4 cup	chopped fresh parsley	50 mL
	Salt and pepper	
1 lb	linguine	500 g
	Freshly grated Parmesan cheese	

• With fork, pierce eggplant all over; wrap in
paper towel and place on plate. Microwave
at High for 8 to 10 minutes or until softened
and skin is wrinkled, turning over halfway
through. Let stand for 10 minutes.

• In 12-cup (3 L) casserole, combine onions,
red pepper, garlic and oil; cover with waxed
paper and microwave at High for 2 minutes
or until softened, stirring once. Add tomatoes
and microwave, covered with waxed paper,
at High for 15 minutes, stirring twice.

• Scoop out eggplant flesh and stir into
tomato mixture along with parsley. Season
with salt and pepper to taste.

• In large pot of boiling salted water, cook
linguine according to package directions or
until al dente (tender but firm); drain. Toss
with tomato sauce mixture and serve. Pass
Parmesan cheese separately. Makes about 4
servings.

Vegetables

Vegetables cooked tender-crisp in the microwave retain more of their bright color and flavor – and their vitamins – than when they are boiled or steamed. Asparagus is a microwave star, especially Asparagus Vinaigrette Mimosa (p. 127). Vegetable combination dishes such as Glazed Carrots and Parsnips (p. 128) and Carrot Coins with Spinach (p. 128) present beautifully on a dinner plate. Even the sturdy potato appears in alluring new styles in recipes for Mexican Couch Potatoes with Salsa (p. 134) and Stuffed Potato Primavera (p. 135). For fresh or frozen vegetable cooking, see the charts we've included on pages 168-69.

VEGETABLE MEDLEY

Colorful vegetables arranged in rings on a platter make a dramatic presentation. Cook all the vegetables at the same time by arranging the longer-cooking denser ones around the outside and faster-cooking ones inside.

1-1/2 cups	cauliflower florets	375 mL
Half	sweet red pepper, cut in 1-inch (2.5 cm) squares	Half
1 cup	snow peas, trimmed	250 mL
1/2 cup	bean sprouts	125 mL
2 tbsp	water	25 mL
2 tbsp	butter	25 mL
2 tbsp	chopped chives	25 mL
1 tbsp	lemon juice	15 mL
	Salt and pepper	

• Around outside of flat 10-inch (25 cm) plate or shallow dish, arrange cauliflower in ring. Arrange ring of red pepper next to cauliflower, then ring of snow peas. Mound bean sprouts in center.
• Sprinkle vegetables with water and cover with vented plastic wrap; microwave at High for 3 to 5 minutes or just until vegetables are tender-crisp, rotating once. Let stand, covered, for 3 minutes.
• Meanwhile, in 1-cup (250 mL) measure, microwave butter and chives at High for 30 to 60 seconds or until butter is melted and chives are softened. Stir in lemon juice.
• Drain water from vegetables without disturbing arrangement; drizzle vegetables with butter mixture. Season with salt and pepper to taste. Makes 4 servings.

For an eye-catching arrangement, mix and match the vegetables in the Vegetable Medley recipe. Remember to put vegetables that take the longest cooking time around the outside edge of the plate. Here are two interesting combinations:
• *1 cup (250 mL) each sliced carrots around the outside, then cauliflower florets, broccoli florets and sliced zucchini in the center.*
• *1-1/2 cups (375 mL) each thinly sliced carrots around the outside, then cubed turnip (1/4-inch/5 mm cubes), and 1 cup (250 mL) trimmed snow peas in the center.*

Vegetable Medley

ACORN SQUASH RINGS STUFFED WITH CRANBERRIES AND APPLES

Present a colorful dish of fresh fall flavors – the perfect accompaniment to Breaded Herb Pork Chops (recipe, p. 66).

1	acorn squash	1
1/4 cup	butter	50 mL
1/2 cup	cranberries	125 mL
1/4 cup	packed brown sugar	50 mL
1/2 cup	finely chopped apple	125 mL
1 tsp	cornstarch	5 mL
2 tsp	cold water	10 mL

• Cut unpeeled squash into 4 rings; remove and discard seeds. Place in shallow dish and set aside.

• In 4-cup (1 L) measure, microwave butter at High for 30 to 45 seconds or until melted. Stir in cranberries and brown sugar. Microwave, covered with vented plastic wrap, at High for 2 to 3 minutes or until skins have popped, stirring once.

• Stir in apple; spoon evenly into center of each squash ring. Cover with vented plastic wrap and microwave at High for 5 to 7 minutes or until squash is tender, rotating halfway through. Drain juices into 1-cup (250 mL) measure and reserve.

• Dissolve cornstarch in cold water; whisk into juices. Microwave at High for 30 to 45 seconds or until mixture boils and thickens slightly, stirring once. Pour over squash rings. Makes 4 servings.

Stuffed Artichokes

STUFFED ARTICHOKES

You'll welcome an encore of turkey in this attractive dish. Artichokes are quickly and easily cooked in a microwave oven.

4	large artichokes (about 14 oz/400 g each)	4
1 tbsp	lemon juice	15 mL
1 tbsp	white wine or water	15 mL
STUFFING:		
1	onion, chopped	1
1	clove garlic, minced	1
2 cups	finely chopped cooked turkey or chicken (3/4 lb/375 g)	500 mL
1/2 cup	sausage meat (1/4 lb/125 g)	125 mL
1/2 cup	fresh bread crumbs*	125 mL
1	egg	1
1/4 cup	chopped fresh parsley	50 mL
1/2 tsp	each salt and dried thyme	2 mL
Pinch	pepper	Pinch

• Break off stems of artichoke; cut off 1 inch (2.5 cm) from tops. Using scissors, cut off tips of leaves. Brush artichokes with lemon juice. Place in shallow dish; cover with vented plastic wrap. Microwave at High for 8 to 10 minutes or until almost tender. Let stand while preparing stuffing.
• **Stuffing:** In bowl, combine onion and garlic; microwave at High for 1 to 1-1/2 minutes or until softened. Stir in turkey, sausage, bread crumbs, egg, parsley, salt, thyme and pepper; mix well and set aside.
• Using spoon, remove and discard center leaves of each artichoke; scrape out fuzzy center and discard. Evenly spoon turkey mixture into hollows. Add wine to baking dish and return artichokes to dish. Cover with waxed paper and microwave at High for 10 to 12 minutes or until stuffing is firm and cooked through. Makes 4 servings.

*Trim crusts from 2 slices white or whole wheat bread; cut bread into cubes and process in food processor or blender until crumbly.

ASPARAGUS VINAIGRETTE MIMOSA

This aristocratic vegetable deserves a special presentation. Press hard-cooked egg white and yolk through a sieve for a pretty white and yellow garnish.

1 lb	asparagus	500 g
2 tbsp	water	25 mL
1	egg	1
1/3 cup	vegetable oil	75 mL
2 tbsp	white wine vinegar	25 mL
1 tsp	Dijon mustard	5 mL
1/4 tsp	salt	1 mL
2 tbsp	chopped fresh parsley	25 mL

• Snap off tough ends of asparagus and discard; peel stems. On round microwaveable serving platter, arrange asparagus with tips toward center. Sprinkle with water; cover with vented plastic wrap and microwave at High for 3 to 5 minutes or just until tender-crisp, rotating platter once. Let stand, covered, for 3 minutes; carefully drain off water and let cool.
• Separate egg into two custard cups (yolk in one, white in the other); pierce yolk and white with toothpick. Cover with vented plastic wrap and microwave at Medium (50%) for 1 to 1-1/2 minutes or until firm. Let stand for 1 minute.
• Whisk together oil, vinegar, mustard and salt; drizzle over asparagus. Press egg yolk and white separately through sieve; arrange egg yolk in ring over asparagus, then ring of egg white. Sprinkle parsley in center. Makes about 4 servings.

VEGETABLE TIPS
• *Wash vegetables well; shake off excess moisture; do not drain. Because many vegetables have a naturally high moisture content, the water clinging to them after washing is often enough for cooking. Fibrous vegetables such as green beans and carrots need additional water (see chart, p. 168).*
• *Frozen vegetables do not require any added water.*
• *Cut vegetables into uniform pieces for more even cooking. The smaller the pieces, the faster they will cook.*
• *Cover vegetables with a tight lid or vented plastic wrap.*
• *Whole vegetables like squash, eggplant, potatoes, yams and beets need their skins pierced before cooking, to allow steam to escape without bursting. Place on paper towels to absorb excess moisture. Arrange like spokes of a wheel; turn over and rotate once during cooking.*
• *Always microwave vegetables at High.*
• *Add salt after cooking to prevent dark, dry spots on food.*
• *Cook vegetables until tender-crisp; remove from microwave and let stand for 3 to 5 minutes.*

BRUSSELS SPROUTS WITH TOASTED ALMONDS

When tender-crisp brussels sprouts are teamed with golden-brown almonds, their wonderful flavor will surprise you. Serve with Sunday Chicken (recipe, p. 84).

1/2 cup	chopped almonds	125 mL
1 lb	brussels sprouts, halved	500 g
1/4 cup	water	50 mL
1 tbsp	butter	15 mL
1 tbsp	lemon juice	15 mL
	Salt and pepper	

• In pie plate or bowl, microwave almonds at High for 2 to 4 minutes or until golden brown, stirring twice. Set aside.
• In 6-cup (1.5 L) casserole, microwave brussels sprouts and water, covered, at High for 6 to 8 minutes or until tender-crisp, stirring once. Drain; stir in butter and lemon juice. Season with salt and pepper to taste. Sprinkle with toasted almonds. Makes 4 servings.

CARROT COINS WITH SPINACH

A perfect foil for Braised Ham with Madeira Sauce (recipe, p. 68), these simple vegetables look and taste wonderful.

1	pkg (10 oz/300 g) spinach	1
3/4 lb	carrots	375 g
1	lemon	1
1 tbsp	butter	15 mL
	Salt and pepper	

• Trim and wash spinach. Place in 12-cup (3 L) casserole with just the water clinging to leaves. Peel and slice carrots diagonally into coins; add to casserole. Using vegetable peeler, remove 4 strips of lemon rind; add to casserole.
• Cover and microwave at High for 5 to 7 minutes or until spinach has wilted and carrots are tender-crisp. Drain well.
• Squeeze 1 tbsp (15 mL) juice from lemon into small bowl; add butter and microwave at High for 30 to 60 seconds or until melted. Pour over vegetables. Season with salt and pepper to taste. Makes about 4 servings.

Your microwave oven does a superb job of steaming vegetables to perfection, with a minimum amount of water. Microwaved vegetables will have vibrant color and fresh-picked flavor and texture. For fresh or frozen vegetable cooking, see our charts on pages 168-69.

GLAZED CARROTS AND PARSNIPS

A hint of ginger and a tang of orange give new life to this perfect autumn dish. Serve alongside Shepherd's Pie (recipe, p. 62).

1/2 lb	carrots (about 3)	250 g
1/2 lb	parsnips (about 3)	250 g
1 tbsp	orange juice	15 mL
1 tbsp	butter	15 mL
2 tsp	liquid honey	10 mL
1/2 tsp	ground ginger	2 mL
	Salt and pepper	

• Peel carrots and parsnips; halve crosswise then cut lengthwise into strips.
• Place in 6-cup (1.5 L) casserole along with 2 tbsp (25 mL) water; microwave at High for 5 to 8 minutes or until tender-crisp, stirring once. Drain and set aside.
• In 1-cup (250 mL) measure, combine orange juice, butter, honey and ginger; microwave at High for 30 to 45 seconds or until butter has melted. Stir into vegetables; season with salt and pepper to taste. Makes about 4 servings.

Herbed Carrots with Onions

HERBED CARROTS WITH ONIONS

Ordinary vegetables become extraordinary in the microwave. Serve this easy combination alongside Lamb Stew with Apricots (recipe, p. 33).

1/4 cup	chopped or thinly sliced onions	50 mL
1	clove garlic, minced	1
1 tbsp	butter	15 mL
1 tbsp	vegetable oil	15 mL
2 cups	sliced carrots	500 mL
1/4 cup	chicken stock	50 mL
	Salt and pepper	
1 tbsp	chopped fresh parsley	15 mL

• In 4-cup (1 L) measure, combine onions, garlic, butter and oil. Cover with vented plastic wrap and microwave at High for 2 minutes or until softened.
• Add carrots and chicken stock; microwave, covered, at High for 4 to 6 minutes or until carrots are just barely tender. Season with salt and pepper to taste. Let stand for 5 minutes.
• Drain off cooking liquid; serve sprinkled with parsley. Makes 4 servings.

STUFFED YELLOW PEPPERS

Buttery rice studded with colorful vegetables makes an attractive and tasty filling for tender sweet peppers. Red or green bell peppers may be used instead of yellow peppers.

3	yellow sweet peppers	3
2 tbsp	water	25 mL
2 tbsp	butter	25 mL
1	clove garlic, chopped	1
2 cups	cooked rice	500 mL
3/4 cup	cooked or canned corn kernels	175 mL
2	green onions, chopped	2
1	tomato, peeled, seeded and chopped	1
1 tbsp	chopped fresh tarragon or parsley	15 mL
	Salt and pepper	

• Halve peppers lengthwise; remove seeds and ribs. On large round dish, arrange peppers cut sides down in 2 tbsp (25 mL) water. Cover with vented plastic wrap and microwave at High for 2 to 4 minutes or until tender-crisp, rotating dish twice. Drain off liquid and invert pepper shells; set aside.
• In 1-cup (250 mL) measure, microwave butter at High for 30 to 45 seconds or until melted. Stir in garlic; cover and microwave at High for 1 minute or until fragrant.
• In small bowl, combine rice, corn, green onions, tomato and tarragon; stir in butter mixture. Season with salt and pepper to taste. Spoon into pepper halves. Cover with waxed paper and microwave at Medium (50%) for 10 to 15 minutes or until peppers are tender, rotating dish three or four times. Let stand, covered, for 2 minutes. Makes 6 servings.

BEET, ENDIVE AND WATERCRESS SALAD

Serve this unusual and pretty salad alongside Ham and Spinach Frittata (recipe, p. 112).

2	beets (1/2 lb/250 g total)	2
1/4 cup	water	50 mL
3	heads Belgian endive	3
2 cups	loosely packed watercress leaves	500 mL
1 tbsp	white wine vinegar	15 mL
1 tbsp	chopped shallots	15 mL
1 tsp	Dijon mustard	5 mL
1/4 tsp	salt	2 mL
Pinch	each granulated sugar and pepper	Pinch
1/4 cup	vegetable oil	50 mL

• In 6-cup (1.5 L) casserole, combine beets with water; cover and microwave at High for 10 to 12 minutes or until tender. Drain and let cool. Slip off skins and slice.
• Remove Belgian endive leaves and arrange around outside of salad bowl or platter. Mound watercress in center; nestle beet slices in watercress.
• In small bowl, whisk together vinegar, shallots, mustard, salt, sugar and pepper; gradually whisk in oil. Drizzle over salad. Makes about 4 servings.

CORN-ON-THE-COB
Once you've tasted sweet and succulent corn-on-the-cob cooked in the microwave, you won't cook corn any other way.
• *Select fresh-picked corn at its peak.*
• *Remove silk; leave cobs in husks and tie with string.*
• *Alternately, place each cob on sheet of plastic wrap. Spread with 1 tbsp (15 mL) butter. Wrap cobs in plastic wrap, twisting ends to seal. (Leave one end loosely twisted to allow excess steam to escape.)*
• *Place in microwave oven like spokes of a wheel with thick end pointing out and tapered end pointing in. This arrangement ensures fast and uniform cooking.*
• *Microwave at High for 2 to 3 minutes per cob (or see chart, p. 168). Let stand for 10 minutes before unwrapping.*

VEGETARIAN CHILI

A lighter-than-usual version of an old favorite.

1 cup	diagonally sliced carrots	250 mL
1 cup	sliced celery	250 mL
1 cup	chopped green onions	250 mL
1 cup	each chopped sweet red and green peppers	250 mL
1/2 cup	sliced green beans	125 mL
1/2 cup	sliced yellow beans	125 mL
1/2 cup	finely chopped leeks	125 mL
1	clove garlic, minced	1
1 tbsp	chili powder	15 mL
1-1/2 tsp	cumin	7 mL
1-1/2 tsp	dried basil	7 mL
1-1/2 tsp	dried oregano	7 mL
1/2 tsp	pepper	2 mL
1	can (28 oz/796 mL) tomatoes (undrained)	1
1	can (19 oz/540 mL) kidney beans, drained and rinsed	1
1/2 cup	freshly grated Parmesan cheese	125 mL

• In 10-cup (2.5 L) bowl, combine carrots, celery, onions, red and green peppers, green and yellow beans, leeks and garlic. Stir in chili powder, cumin, basil, oregano and pepper.
• Drain tomatoes, reserving juice; chop tomatoes and set aside. Add juice to vegetable mixture; cover with vented plastic wrap and microwave at High for 10 to 12 minutes or until vegetables are tender-crisp, stirring several times.
• Add tomatoes and kidney beans; microwave at High, covered, for 2 minutes or until heated through. Spoon into 4 serving dishes; sprinkle with Parmesan. Microwave at High for 30 seconds or until cheese begins to melt. Makes 4 to 6 servings.

SPAGHETTI SQUASH WITH CLAM AND MUSHROOM SAUCE

A 3-1/2 lb (1.5 kg) squash gives about 6 cups (1.5 L) spaghetti-like strands. If a larger squash is used, toss extra squash strands with a little vinaigrette. Cover and refrigerate to serve later, or the next day, as a salad. If you like, substitute Easy Tomato Sauce (recipe, p. 28) for the Clam and Mushroom Sauce.

1	spaghetti squash (about 3-1/2 lb/ 1.5 kg)	1
	Salt and pepper	
2 tbsp	butter	25 mL
1 cup	sliced mushrooms	250 mL
2 tbsp	chopped green onion	25 mL
2 tbsp	all-purpose flour	25 mL
1	can (5 oz/142 g) clams (undrained)	1
1 cup	light cream	250 mL
1/4 cup	white wine	50 mL

• Pierce squash in several places; place on double thickness of paper towels and microwave at High for 10 minutes, turning over halfway through. Halve squash lengthwise; remove and discard seeds.
• Cover squash halves with vented plastic wrap and microwave at High for 12 to 15 minutes or until tender, rotating squash twice. Let stand for 2 minutes. With fork, remove spaghetti-like strands of squash; place in bowl and season with salt and pepper to taste. Cover and keep warm.
• In 4-cup (1 L) measure, microwave butter at High for 30 seconds or until melted. Stir in mushrooms and green onion; microwave at High, uncovered, for 2 to 3 minutes or until softened, stirring once. Stir in flour.
• Drain clams, reserving 1/3 cup (75 mL) juice. Gradually stir clam juice, cream and wine into mushroom mixture; microwave at High, uncovered, for 2 to 4 minutes or until mixture comes to boil and thickens, stirring twice.
• Stir in clams; microwave at High for 1 minute or until heated through. Season with salt and pepper to taste. Pour over spaghetti squash. Makes 4 to 6 servings.

HERBED POTATO STICKS

Cooking the potatoes in butter or oil instead of water captures their full flavor. Gentle stirring during cooking ensures evenly cooked vegetables.

1/4 cup	finely chopped onion	50 mL
2 tbsp	olive oil	25 mL
1 tbsp	butter	15 mL
1	clove garlic, minced	1
3 tbsp	chopped fresh parsley	50 mL
1 tbsp	chopped fresh basil (or 1/2 tsp/2 mL dried)	15 mL
1 tsp	chili powder	5 mL
1/4 tsp	salt	1 mL
Pinch	pepper	Pinch
4	large potatoes	4

• In 8-cup (2 L) baking dish, combine onion, oil, butter and garlic; microwave at High for 1-1/2 to 2 minutes or until onion is softened, stirring once. Stir in parsley, basil, chili powder, salt and pepper. Set aside.
• Wash and scrub potatoes well. Halve lengthwise; cut each half into 4 sticks. Add to baking dish; toss to coat evenly. Cover and microwave at High for 10 to 12 minutes or until fork-tender, stirring halfway through. To serve, spoon onion mixture over potatoes. Makes 4 servings.

*WHOLE RUTABAGAS
To cook rutabagas, pierce all over with a small knife; place on paper towel (to absorb dripping from wax coating). Microwave at High for 10 to 14 minutes (timing will depend on size), or until tender when pierced with a knife. Wrap completely in foil and let stand for 15 to 20 minutes. Then peel, mash and season to taste. This eliminates difficult cutting.*

Spaghetti Squash with Clam and Mushroom Sauce

BRAISED POTATOES

These tender, savory potatoes are a satisfying side dish for Choucroute Garnie (recipe, p. 70).

1 lb	potatoes, peeled and sliced	500 g
1	onion, thinly sliced	1
2 tbsp	butter	25 mL
1/2 cup	chicken stock	125 mL
	Salt and pepper	

• In 10-inch (25 cm) pie plate, combine potatoes and onion. Dot with butter and pour chicken stock over. Season with salt and pepper to taste. Cover with vented plastic wrap and microwave at High for 10 to 15 minutes or until potatoes are tender, stirring halfway through. Set aside until just before serving. To reheat, cover and microwave at High for 2 minutes or until heated through. Makes 4 servings.

MEXICAN COUCH POTATOES WITH SALSA

Here is an entirely new and original approach to the humble baked potato.

4	large baking potatoes (2 lb/1 kg total)	4
1/2 cup	cottage cheese	125 mL
1/2 cup	sour cream	125 mL
1/2 cup	shredded Monterey Jack or Cheddar cheese	125 mL
1/4 cup	chopped green onion	50 mL
1 tbsp	chopped pickled jalapeño peppers	15 mL
	Salt and pepper	
SALSA:		
1 tbsp	vegetable oil	15 mL
1	onion, chopped	1
1	clove garlic, minced	1
1	sweet green pepper, chopped	1
1 cup	chopped drained canned tomatoes	250 mL
2 tbsp	chopped fresh coriander or parsley	25 mL
Dash	hot pepper sauce	Dash
	Salt and pepper	

• **Salsa:** In 4-cup (1 L) measure, combine oil, onion and garlic; microwave at High for 1 to 2 minutes or until onion is tender, stirring once. Add green pepper, tomatoes, coriander, hot pepper sauce, and salt and pepper to taste; microwave at High for 4 minutes or until heated through and green pepper is tender, stirring once. Let cool.
• Prick potatoes in several places; arrange in circle 1 inch (2.5 cm) apart on paper towel. Microwave at High for 10 to 15 minutes or until tender, turning over and rearranging once. Let stand for 5 minutes.
• Cut thin slice from top of each potato and scoop out pulp, leaving 1/4-inch (5 mm) thick shell. In bowl, mash potato lightly; stir in cottage cheese, sour cream, 1/4 cup (50 mL) of the Monterey Jack, green onion, jalapeño, and salt and pepper to taste. Spoon evenly into potato shells; arrange in circle on plate. Sprinkle with remaining cheese; microwave at Medium (50%) for 8 minutes or until heated through, rotating dish once. Serve with salsa. Makes 4 servings.

Arrange potatoes in a circle at least 1 inch (2.5 cm) apart on a paper towel.

SCALLOPED POTATOES

Scalloped potatoes turn out perfectly if you cook the sauce first, then add the potatoes.

3 tbsp	butter	50 mL
1	onion, finely chopped	1
1 tbsp	all-purpose flour	15 mL
1-1/2 cups	milk	375 mL
2 tbsp	chopped fresh parsley	25 mL
1 tsp	salt	5 mL
1/2 tsp	dry mustard	2 mL
1/4 tsp	pepper	1 mL
4 cups	thinly sliced peeled potatoes (about 4 potatoes)	1 L

• In 4-cup (1 L) measure, microwave 1 tbsp (15 mL) of the butter at High for 30 to 40 seconds or until melted. Stir in onion; microwave at High for 2 to 4 minutes or until softened, stirring once. Blend in flour.
• Gradually whisk in milk; microwave at High for 5 to 8 minutes or until mixture comes to boil and thickens slightly, whisking 3 times. Whisk in parsley, salt, mustard and pepper.
• In 8-cup (2 L) casserole, combine potatoes and sauce; dot with remaining butter. Cover and microwave at Medium-High (70%) for 20 to 25 minutes or until potatoes are tender, stirring 3 times. Let stand, covered, for 3 minutes. Makes 4 to 6 servings.

To make a cheesy version of Scalloped Potatoes, add 1/2 cup (125 mL) shredded Cheddar cheese to the sauce before mixing with the potatoes. Top with an additional 1/2 cup (125 mL) shredded Cheddar before covering the casserole and letting stand.

Mexican Couch Potatoes with Salsa

STUFFED POTATO PRIMAVERA

If you prefer a drier potato, place it on a double thickness of paper towelling in your microwave. After cooking time, wrap in a tea towel while preparing the topping. If you like a steamier potato, wrap it in foil while preparing the topping.

4	large baking potatoes	4
TOPPING:		
1 tbsp	butter	15 mL
1 tbsp	all-purpose flour	15 mL
1 cup	milk	250 mL
1 tsp	Dijon mustard	5 mL
	Salt and pepper	
1 cup	shredded Swiss or Cheddar cheese	250 mL
1-1/2 cups	cubed cooked ham	375 mL
1-1/2 cups	sliced zucchini	375 mL
2 tbsp	water	25 mL

• Scrub potatoes and prick with fork; arrange in microwave at least 1 inch (2.5 cm) apart in circle. Microwave at High for 10 to 12 minutes or until potatoes give slightly when squeezed, turning over halfway through and rearranging once. Wrap each potato snugly in foil or tea towel while preparing topping.

• **Topping:** In 4-cup (1 L) measure or bowl, microwave butter at High for 15 seconds or until melted. Stir in flour until smooth; microwave at High for 30 seconds. Gradually stir in milk until smooth; microwave at High for 3 to 4 minutes or until thickened and boiling, stirring every minute.

• Stir in mustard; season with salt and pepper to taste. Add cheese, stirring until melted. Fold in ham; set aside.

• In dish, combine zucchini and water; microwave at High for 2 to 3 minutes or until tender-crisp, stirring once. Drain and stir zucchini into sauce; microwave at High for 1 to 2 minutes or until heated through.

• Cut deep cross in top of each potato; squeeze lightly to open. Spoon topping over each potato. Makes 4 servings.

Quick Breads, Cakes and Squares

Let's be honest. There are limitations to baking in the microwave oven. For yeast breads and cookies, we recommend you use your conventional oven. But many quick breads – such as muffins, biscuits and scones – and cakes can be made quickly in the microwave. You can enjoy fresh Nutty Orange Bran Muffins (p. 137) each morning, for example, with batter you can keep in the refrigerator. Our Superfast Brownies (p. 145) and Crunchy Cocoa-Cinnamon Coffee Cake (p. 142) are much better than store-bought. And the Oatmeal Chocolate Squares (p. 37) are so easy even kids can make them.

• *Round and ring-shaped dishes produce the best results. If you use a square dish, be careful that edges and corners are not overdone before center is cooked. Prevent this by shielding corners with small, smooth triangles of aluminum foil for the first half of cooking time. Remember to remove the foil for the final cooking.*

• *Microwaving causes cakes to rise higher, so fill baking dish only half full.*

• *Let cake batters stand 5 to 10 minutes before cooking, to prevent uneven top.*

• *If your microwaved cake has wet spots on the bottom, try elevating cake dish on a roasting rack or inverted saucer for more even cooking next time.*

• *Rotate dish a half-turn at least once during cooking time unless oven has built-in or portable turntable.*

• *Bake cakes uncovered; steamed puddings covered with vented plastic wrap.*

• *Check for doneness at minimum baking time; overcooking toughens cakes. Test with toothpick; if it comes out clean and most of the moistness on top has disappeared, cake is ready.*

• *Generally, baked goods should stand, covered, directly on flat, heatproof surface for standing time indicated in recipe. Uncover and transfer to cooling rack until completely cooled.*

Nutty Orange Bran Muffins; Cornmeal Biscuits

NUTTY ORANGE BRAN MUFFINS

A fruity taste and nutty texture combine in this satisfying muffin. Cook the batter right away, or keep it for up to 2 weeks in the fridge and enjoy a fresh hot muffin every day. To cook 1 muffin, microwave at High for 45 seconds; 2 muffins for 1 minute; 4 muffins for 1-1/2 minutes.

2/3 cup	all-purpose flour	150 mL
1/4 cup	natural bran	50 mL
1/4 cup	packed brown sugar	50 mL
1/2 tsp	baking soda	2 mL
Pinch	salt	Pinch
1/3 cup	chopped dates	75 mL
1	egg	1
1/3 cup	vegetable oil	75 mL
1/4 cup	buttermilk	50 mL
1/4 cup	fancy molasses	50 mL
2 tbsp	orange juice concentrate	25 mL

• In large bowl, combine flour, bran, sugar, baking soda and salt; mix in dates. In separate bowl, beat together egg, oil, buttermilk, molasses, orange juice concentrate and rind; stir into flour mixture just until blended.

• Line 12 muffin or custard cups with 2 paper liners each. Divide batter among cups, filling no more than half full.

• **Topping:** Combine walnuts, sugar and cinnamon; sprinkle evenly over muffins. Microwave, 6 muffins at a time, at High for 2 minutes or until tester inserted in centers comes out clean, rotating once. Let stand on flat surface for 3 minutes. Makes 12 muffins.

CORNMEAL BISCUITS

Treat your family to savory Cornmeal Biscuits instead of toast or muffins.

3/4 cup	all-purpose flour	175 mL
1/4 cup	cornmeal	50 mL
1/4 cup	freshly grated Parmesan cheese	50 mL
1-1/2 tsp	baking powder	7 mL
1/4 tsp	salt	1 mL
1/4 tsp	paprika	1 mL
Pinch	cayenne pepper	Pinch
1/4 cup	butter	50 mL
1/3 cup	finely chopped sweet red pepper	75 mL
1/4 cup	sour cream	50 mL
3 tbsp	milk	50 mL
1	egg yolk	1

• In bowl, combine flour, cornmeal, Parmesan cheese, baking powder, salt, paprika and cayenne. With pastry blender, cut in butter until mixture resembles coarse crumbs. Stir in red pepper.

• Combine sour cream, milk and egg yolk; stir into flour mixture to form soft dough. Turn out onto lightly floured surface and knead into ball.

• Roll out dough to 1/4-inch (5 mm) thickness. With 2-1/2-inch (6 cm) cutter, cut into 8 rounds. Arrange around outside of 12-inch (30 cm) round flat plate or pie plate; microwave at Medium (50%) for 6 to 8 minutes, rotating or rearranging twice or until puffed and firm to the touch. Let stand directly on counter, for 5 minutes. Transfer to rack and let cool completely. Makes 8 biscuits.

CHEESE AND CORNMEAL SCONES

Warm cheesy scones are perfect lunch partners for soup and salad. (photo, p. 21)

3/4 cup	all-purpose flour	175 mL
1/4 cup	cornmeal	50 mL
1-1/2 tsp	baking powder	7 mL
1/4 tsp	salt	1 mL
2 tbsp	butter	25 mL
1/2 cup	shredded old Cheddar cheese	125 mL
1	egg yolk	1
1/3 cup	milk	75 mL
	Paprika	

• In bowl, combine flour, cornmeal, baking powder and salt. Cut in butter and cheese until mixture resembles coarse crumbs. Beat together egg yolk and milk; stir into flour mixture to form dough.
• Turn out onto lightly floured surface; knead into ball. Roll out dough into 7-inch (18 cm) circle. Cut into 6 wedges. Sprinkle lightly with paprika. Place on lightly greased 10-inch (25 cm) pie plate; separate wedges slightly. Microwave at Medium (50%) for 6 minutes or until puffed and firm to the touch, rotating dish every 2 minutes. Let stand directly on flat surface for 5 minutes. Serve warm. Makes 6 scones.

GINGERBREAD

Serve this cake plain with whipped cream or a dusting of icing sugar, or warm with softened vanilla ice cream.

1/2 cup	buttermilk	125 mL
1/4 cup	molasses	50 mL
3 tbsp	vegetable oil	50 mL
1	egg	1
1 cup	all-purpose flour	250 mL
1/3 cup	packed brown sugar	75 mL
1 tsp	ginger	5 mL
1/2 tsp	baking soda	2 mL
1/4 tsp	baking powder	1 mL
1/4 tsp	nutmeg	1 mL
1/4 tsp	allspice	1 mL

• In bowl, combine buttermilk, molasses, oil and egg. Stir together flour, sugar, ginger, baking soda, baking powder, nutmeg and allspice; add to molasses mixture and stir until well blended.
• Pour batter into 8-cup (2 L) lightly greased ring mould. Microwave at High for 4-1/2 to 6-1/2 minutes or until tester inserted in center of cake comes out clean, rotating dish twice.
• Let stand on flat surface for 10 minutes. Run knife around outside edge and turn out onto serving plate. Makes 8 servings.

PEAR UPSIDE-DOWN GINGERBREAD

You can present this fragrant, spicy cake with a mound of whipped cream or ice cream for added luxury.

3	pears	3
1/4 cup	packed brown sugar	50 mL
2 tbsp	lemon juice	25 mL
1 tsp	cornstarch	5 mL
3/4 tsp	cinnamon	4 mL
	Gingerbread batter (recipe above)	

• Peel, core and slice pears into 8-inch (2 L) square baking dish, greased on bottom. In small bowl, combine sugar, lemon juice, cornstarch and cinnamon. Pour over pears and cover with vented plastic wrap. Microwave at High for 3 to 4 minutes or until pears are tender, stirring once during cooking. Rearrange pear slices evenly over bottom of dish.
• Pour prepared Gingerbread batter over pears, spreading evenly. Microwave at High, uncovered, for 6 to 7 minutes or until surface is almost dry and top has a small moist spot, rotating dish once during cooking. Let stand for 5 minutes. Invert onto serving plate if desired Makes 8 servings.

Quick breads, cakes and bar cookies have a different appearance when made in the microwave oven. They don't form a crust or brown, so choose recipes with built-in browning, like brown sugar, spices, molasses, chocolate, or whole wheat flour. Overcooking can occur with only 30 seconds too long in the microwave, so watch dishes carefully and check for doneness often.

TIPS TO ENHANCE THE APPEARANCE OF BAKED GOODS
• *Top with icing sugar, chopped nuts, coconut (toasted or plain), cinnamon-sugar, frosting or sauces.*
• *Substitute brown sugar for granulated sugar. Dark brown sugar adds more color than light brown sugar.*
• *Substitute whole wheat flour for half of the all-purpose flour in a recipe.*

Raisin and Spice Cake

RAISIN AND SPICE CAKE

*A piece of this dark spicy cake, made in
minutes in the microwave, is the ideal choice
to serve with a pot of hot tea in the afternoon.
Brown Sugar Frosting (recipe, p. 141) is
delicious on this cake. Be sure the cake is cool
before frosting.*

1-1/2 cup	raisins	375 mL
3/4 cup	packed dark brown sugar	175 mL
3/4 cup	water	175 mL
1/2 cup	shortening	125 mL
1/4 cup	dark molasses	50 mL
1 tsp	cinnamon	5 mL
1/2 tsp	nutmeg	2 mL
1/4 tsp	cloves	1 mL
1-3/4 cup	all-purpose flour	425 mL
1 tsp	baking soda	5 mL

• In 8-cup (2 L) measure, combine raisins,
sugar, water, shortening, molasses,
cinnamon, nutmeg and cloves; microwave at
High for 5 to 7 minutes or until boiling. Let
cool to lukewarm.
• Mix together flour and baking soda; stir
into liquid mixture. Lightly grease bottom of
8-inch (2 L) square dish; pour in batter.
Shield corners with foil.
• Microwave at High for 4 minutes, rotating
dish each minute; remove shields. Microwave
at High for 2 to 3 minutes longer or until
tester inserted in center comes out clean,
rotating dish one-quarter turn each minute.
Let cool on counter.

CHOCOLATE CAKE

This recipe can be used for one 8-inch (20 cm) round cake or 12 cupcakes. Spread while hot with Crunchy Topping (recipe follows) or cool and frost with Brown Sugar Frosting (recipe follows).

2 oz	unsweetened chocolate	60 g
3 tbsp	butter	50 mL
1 cup	all-purpose flour	250 mL
3/4 cup	lightly packed brown sugar	175 mL
1/2 tsp	baking soda	2 mL
1/4 tsp	salt	1 mL
3/4 cup	sour cream	175 mL
1	egg, beaten	1
1/2 tsp	vanilla	2 mL

• In custard cup, combine chocolate and butter; cover with vented plastic wrap and microwave at Medium (50%) for 1-1/2 minutes or until almost melted. Stir until chocolate has completely melted; set aside and let cool slightly.
• In bowl, stir together flour, sugar, baking soda and salt. Mix together sour cream, egg and vanilla; blend into dry ingredients and mix with wooden spoon until smooth. Add chocolate mixture and beat until well blended and creamy.
• Pour into greased or waxed paper-lined 8-inch (20 cm) round cake dish; set on inverted saucer in oven. Let stand for 5 minutes.
• Microwave at Medium (50%), uncovered, for 4 minutes, rotating dish twice. Microwave at High for 2 to 4 minutes or just until moistness has disappeared from surface of cake and tester inserted in center comes out clean.
• Let stand directly on counter for 10 minutes. Turn out onto wire rack, or leave in dish on rack, to cool completely.

Chocolate Cupcakes with Crunchy Topping and Brown Sugar Frosting; Carrot Cake

VARIATION:

CHOCOLATE CUPCAKES:

• Spoon half of the batter into 6 double paper-lined custard cups or cupcake moulds. Microwave at Medium (50%) for 3 to 5 minutes or until moistness has disappeared from surface of cakes and tester inserted in centers comes out clean, rotating once. If using individual custard cups, remove from oven as each finishes baking. Let stand directly on counter for 5 minutes. Remove to wire rack and remove extra paper liners (which will be wet). Repeat with remaining batter, stirring before filling cupcake moulds. Makes 12 cupcakes.

CRUNCHY TOPPING:

Make this topping while the cake or cupcakes are standing; then spoon on top of the cake while warm, gently spreading to the edges.

1/2 cup	packed brown sugar	125 mL
1/2 cup	flaked coconut	125 mL
1/4 cup	chopped nuts	50 mL
3 tbsp	butter	50 mL
1 tbsp	milk	15 mL

• In 4-cup (1 L) measure, combine sugar, coconut, nuts, butter and milk; microwave at High, uncovered, for 2 to 3 minutes or until thick and bubbly, stirring twice. Makes enough for one 8-inch (20 cm) round cake or 12 cupcakes.

BROWN SUGAR FROSTING:

Try this creamy icing on chocolate cake or cupcakes.

1/3 cup	packed brown sugar	75 mL
2 tbsp	butter	25 mL
2 tbsp	milk	25 mL
1-1/4 cups	sifted icing sugar	300 mL
1/2 tsp	vanilla	2 mL

• In bowl, combine brown sugar, butter and milk; microwave at High for 45 to 60 seconds or until butter has melted, sugar is dissolved and mixture boils.
• Stir in icing sugar and vanilla; let cool to lukewarm. Beat until thick enough to spread but not grainy. Mixture should hold imprint of spoon. Makes enough for one 8-inch (20 cm) round cake or 12 cupcakes.

CHOCOLATE CAKE TIP
Line a round dish with waxed paper if turning the cake out of the dish after baking. Otherwise, a light greasing is enough for easy cutting and serving. If baking cupcakes, use 2 cupcake paper liners for each cupcake to absorb excess moisture as they cook.

CARROT CAKE

Pineapple adds interesting flavor to this moist, pleasantly spiced cake.

3/4 cup	all-purpose flour	175 mL
1/2 cup	whole wheat flour	125 mL
1 tsp	baking powder	5 mL
1 tsp	cinnamon	5 mL
1/2 tsp	salt	2 mL
1/4 tsp	nutmeg	1 mL
2	eggs	2
1/2 cup	vegetable oil	125 mL
1/2 cup	granulated sugar	125 mL
1/2 cup	packed brown sugar	125 mL
1-1/2 cups	grated raw carrots	375 mL
1/2 cup	raisins	125 mL
1/2 cup	drained crushed pineapple	125 mL

• Combine all-purpose and whole wheat flours, baking powder, cinnamon, salt and nutmeg; set aside.
• In large bowl, beat together eggs and oil until blended; beat in granulated and brown sugars, until light, about 3 minutes. Add carrots, raisins and pineapple; mix well. Add dry ingredients, stirring to mix well.
• Pour batter into greased 8-cup (2 L) ring mould. Microwave at Medium (50%) for 6 minutes, rotating pan twice. Microwave at High for 4 to 6 minutes or until tester inserted in center of cake comes out clean, rotating pan twice.
• Let stand on flat surface for 15 minutes; turn out cake onto wire rack to let cool completely.

CRUNCHY COCOA-CINNAMON COFFEE CAKE

If you haven't tried making a coffee cake in the microwave, this delectable concoction, flavored with cocoa and cinnamon, will astonish and delight you.

1	egg	1
1	egg yolk	1
3/4 cup	packed brown sugar	175 mL
3/4 cup	sour cream	175 mL
1/2 cup	vegetable oil	125 mL
1 tsp	vanilla	5 mL
1-1/2 cups	all-purpose flour	375 mL
3/4 tsp	baking powder	4 mL
3/4 tsp	baking soda	4 mL
1/2 tsp	cinnamon	2 mL
1/4 tsp	salt	1 mL
TOPPING:		
1/3 cup	packed brown sugar	75 mL
3 tbsp	all-purpose flour	50 mL
3 tbsp	unsweetened cocoa powder	50 mL
1/2 tsp	cinnamon	2 mL
3 tbsp	butter	50 mL
3/4 cup	chopped walnuts or pecans	175 mL

• In large bowl, beat together egg, yolk and sugar until well blended; beat in sour cream, oil and vanilla. Stir together flour, baking powder, baking soda, cinnamon and salt; stir into egg mixture.

• **Topping:** In bowl, stir together sugar, flour, cocoa and cinnamon. With pastry blender or 2 knives, cut in butter until crumbly; stir in nuts.

• Spread half of the batter in ungreased 8-inch (2 L) square baking dish; sprinkle with half of the topping. Repeat with remaining batter and topping. Shield corners of dish with foil triangles; place on inverted saucer in oven. Microwave at Medium (50%) for 6 minutes, rotating dish once; remove foil. Microwave at High for 2 to 4 minutes or until tester inserted in center comes out clean, rotating dish once. Let stand on flat surface for 10 minutes before serving warm.

Crunchy Cocoa-Cinnamon Coffee Cake

BLUEBERRY-LEMON UPSIDE-DOWN CAKE

This quick and easy family-style cake has a blueberry-glazed top. When fresh blueberries are available, simply mix the topping ingredients together and spoon into a 9-inch (2 L) ring mould. Top with the cake batter and proceed as directed below.

BLUEBERRY TOPPING:

1-1/2 cups	frozen blueberries	375 mL
3 tbsp	granulated sugar	50 mL
3 tbsp	lemon juice	50 mL

CAKE:

1	egg	1
1	egg yolk	1
3/4 cup	packed brown sugar	175 mL
3/4 cup	sour cream	175 mL
1/2 cup	vegetable oil	125 mL
1 tbsp	each grated lemon rind and lemon juice	15 mL
1 tsp	vanilla	5 mL
1-1/2 cups	all-purpose flour	375 mL
3/4 tsp	baking powder	4 mL
3/4 tsp	baking soda	4 mL
1/4 tsp	salt	1 mL

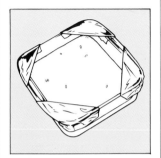

Shield the corners of a square baking dish with aluminum foil triangles to prevent overcooking.

• **Blueberry Topping:** In 8-cup (2 L) ring mould, combine blueberries, sugar and lemon juice. Microwave at High for 2 minutes or until blueberries are thawed; set aside.
• **Cake:** In large bowl, beat together egg, egg yolk and sugar until blended; beat in sour cream, oil, lemon rind, lemon juice and vanilla. Stir together flour, baking powder, baking soda and salt; blend into egg mixture.
• Spoon batter evenly over blueberry mixture. Microwave at Medium (50%) for 5 minutes, rotating pan once. Microwave at High for 2 minutes or until tester inserted in center comes out clean and cake is firm to the touch. Let stand on flat surface for 10 minutes. Run knife around edges to loosen and turn out onto serving platter. Let cool completely.

BANANA NUT CAKE

Contrary to all you've learned about cakes baked in a conventional oven, microwaved cake batters will not fall if you open the oven door and move/rotate the dish several times for even cooking.

1-1/4 cups	all-purpose flour	300 mL
1 tsp	baking powder	5 mL
1/2 tsp	baking soda	2 mL
1/4 tsp	salt	1 mL
1/4 cup	butter	50 mL
3/4 cup	packed brown sugar	175 mL
1	egg	1
1/2 tsp	vanilla	2 mL
1/2 cup	mashed ripe banana	125 mL
1/2 cup	soured milk* or buttermilk	125 mL
1/2 cup	chopped nuts	125 mL

• Combine flour, baking powder, baking soda and salt; set aside.
• In large bowl, cream butter with sugar; beat in egg and vanilla. Mix together banana and sour milk; add to creamed mixture alternately with dry ingredients, making 3 additions of dry and 2 of liquid ingredients. Stir in nuts.
• Pour into lightly greased 8-cup (2 L) ring mould; place on inverted saucer in oven. Microwave at Medium (50%) for 6 minutes, rotating pan twice. Microwave at High for 3 to 5 minutes or until cake tester inserted in center of cake comes out clean, rotating dish twice.
• Let stand on flat surface for 15 minutes; turn out cake onto rack and let cool.

*To sour milk, place 1 tsp (5 mL) lemon juice or vinegar in measuring cup; add milk to the 1/2 cup (125 mL) level and let stand for 5 minutes, then stir.

DATE AND RAISIN SQUARES

These old-fashioned squares are easy to make in the microwave. Be sure to try the Granola Date variation.

FILLING:

1/2 lb	dates, cut up (about 1-1/3 cup/ 325 mL)	250 g
1 cup	(approx) water	250 mL
1/2 cup	raisins	125 mL

CRUMB LAYERS:

1 cup	rolled oats	250 mL
1 cup	all-purpose flour	250 mL
1 cup	lightly packed dark brown sugar	250 mL
1/2 tsp	baking powder	2 mL
1/4 tsp	salt	1 mL
1/2 cup	butter	125 mL

• **Filling:** In 4-cup (1 L) measure, combine dates, water and raisins. Cover with vented plastic wrap and microwave at High for 4 to 6 minutes or until boiling, stirring every 2 minutes. Watch carefully, adding up to 2 tbsp (25 mL) additional water, if mixture is drying before dates are soft. Let stand, covered, for 5 minutes. Uncover and let cool to lukewarm, stirring occasionally.

• **Crumb Layers:** Meanwhile, in bowl, mix together rolled oats, flour, sugar, baking powder and salt. With pastry blender or fingers, cut in butter until mixture is crumbly.

• Pat half of the crumb mixture into 8-inch (2 L) square dish. Spread with filling; top with remaining crumb mixture, patting down evenly. Microwave at Medium-High (70%) for 9 minutes, rotating dish every 3 minutes.

• Cover with foil and let stand directly on countertop for 10 minutes. Uncover and let stand on rack to cool completely. Cut into squares to serve. Makes 25 squares. Store Date and Raisin Squares covered tightly with foil or plastic wrap.

VARIATION:

GRANOLA DATE BARS:

• Omit raisins in filling. Substitute 1-1/2 cups (375 mL) Granola (recipe, p. 164) for rolled oats. Reduce dark brown sugar to 1/2 cup (125 mL).

(Left to right) Pumpkin Ginger Squares; Superfast Brownies; Date and Raisin Squares

PUMPKIN GINGER SQUARES

Pumpkin and ginger are a wonderful flavor combination. Freeze any remaining pumpkin purée (whether commercial or homemade) in 1/2-cup (125 mL) amounts for making these squares again.

1/3 cup	butter	75 mL
1-1/2 cups	gingersnap crumbs (16 to 18 cookies)	375 mL
8 oz	cream cheese, softened	250 g
1/2 cup	pumpkin purée	125 mL
2	eggs	2
1/2 cup	packed brown sugar	125 mL
1 tbsp	chopped candied ginger	15 mL
1/2 tsp	cinnamon or pumpkin pie spice	2 mL

• In 8-inch square (2 L) cake pan, microwave butter at High for 1-1/2 to 2 minutes or until melted; stir in crumbs. Set aside 1/4 cup (50 mL) of the crumb mixture for topping. Pat remaining crumbs into bottom of pan; microwave at High, uncovered, for 2 minutes. Set aside.

• In mixing bowl, beat cream cheese until smooth. Mix in pumpkin, eggs, sugar, ginger and cinnamon just until combined. Pour over crumb base and sprinkle with reserved crumbs. Microwave at Medium (50%), uncovered, for 12 to 16 minutes or until center is almost set, rotating pan twice.

• Cover and let stand on counter for 10 minutes. Uncover and let cool to room temperature, then refrigerate until thoroughly chilled before cutting into squares.

You can substitute chocolate chips (semisweet, milk chocolate, or orange or peppermint flavored) for the chocolate in Superfast Brownies. Use one package (175 g), reserving 1/4 cup (50 mL) chips to use in the icing.

SUPERFAST BROWNIES

Fast to make and fast to disappear from the plate, rich chewy, nutty brownies are an extra-special treat, frosted with smooth chocolate icing. Kids will love to make them – and eat them!

1/4 lb	bittersweet or semisweet chocolate	125 g
1/2 cup	butter	125 mL
2/3 cup	granulated sugar	150 mL
2	eggs	2
1 tsp	vanilla	5 mL
3/4 cup	all-purpose flour	175 mL
1/2 tsp	baking powder	2 mL
1/4 tsp	salt	1 mL
1/2 cup	chopped walnuts	125 mL
ICING:		
2 oz	bittersweet or semisweet chocolate	60 g
1 cup	icing sugar, sifted	250 mL
3 tbsp	butter, softened	50 mL
1/2 tsp	vanilla	2 mL

• In 2-cup (500 mL) measure, microwave chocolate with butter at Medium (50%) for 3 to 4 minutes or until melted, stirring once. Stir and let cool slightly.

• In bowl, beat sugar with eggs; blend in cooled chocolate mixture and vanilla. Combine flour, baking powder and salt; blend into chocolate mixture. Stir in walnuts. Spread in ungreased 8-inch (2 L) square baking dish; shield corners with foil. Microwave at High for 4-1/2 to 5 minutes or until top is no longer sticky and tester inserted in center comes out clean, rotating dish once. Let stand on countertop for 10 minutes. Set on rack and let cool completely.

• **Icing:** In small bowl, microwave chocolate at Medium-High (70%) for 2 minutes or until melted, stirring once. Let cool slightly. Gradually beat icing sugar into butter; beat in chocolate until well blended. Stir in vanilla. Spread over brownies. Cut into squares.

Desserts

There's no better way to end a meal than with a sophisticated yet simple dessert. But when it's a challenge just to get dinner to the table, who has time to make dessert? You do. With the help of your microwave oven, you can create quick and luscious sauces (pp. 160-61) to serve over fresh berries, fruits, ice cream or cake. Or serve tasty puddings like Creamy Rice Pudding (p. 153) or Chocolate Mocha Pudding (p. 152). Even no-bake pies, cheesecakes, mousses and poached desserts can be made when time is limited. Here are some delights to tempt the palate of every dessert lover.

KIWI LIME PIE

Cool and refreshing, this luscious mixture of kiwi fruit and lime juice makes a special dessert to serve on a summer night.

CRUST:		
1/4 cup	butter	50 mL
1 cup	graham wafer crumbs	250 mL
2 tbsp	packed brown sugar	25 mL
FILLING:		
1	small kiwi fruit, peeled	1
3	eggs	3
1 cup	granulated sugar	250 mL
1/2 cup	lime juice	125 mL
1 tsp	grated lime rind	5 mL
1/4 cup	butter, melted	50 mL
2 tbsp	cornstarch	25 mL
3/4 cup	whipping cream	175 mL
GARNISH:		
	Kiwi fruit slices	

- **Crust:** In 9-inch (23 cm) pie plate, microwave butter at High for 35 to 40 seconds or until melted. Add graham wafer crumbs and sugar; mix well. Press evenly over bottom and sides of pie plate. Microwave at High, uncovered, for 2 minutes. Set aside.
- **Filling:** In food processor or blender, process kiwi until smooth; transfer to 4-cup (1 L) measure. Whisk in eggs, sugar, 1/3 cup (75 mL) of the lime juice, lime rind and butter until smooth; microwave at Medium (50%) for 6 to 8 minutes or until thickened, whisking every 2 minutes.
- Dissolve cornstarch in remaining lime juice; whisk into lime mixture and microwave at Medium (50%) for 2 to 4 minutes or until thickened, whisking every minute. Let cool; refrigerate until chilled, stirring occasionally.
- Transfer mixture to large bowl. Whip cream until stiff and fold into lime mixture; spoon into prepared crust. Refrigerate until set. Garnish with kiwi slices.

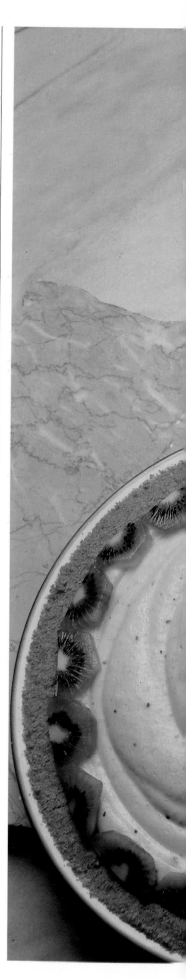

Kiwi Lime Pie; Strawberry Mousse Pie (p. 21)

MARGARITA PIE

Here is a light dessert that is the perfect finale for a Mexican meal. Garnish the pie with chocolate curls or grated chocolate, if you like.

CRUST:

1/2 cup	butter	125 mL
1-1/4 cups	pretzel crumbs	300 mL
1/4 cup	granulated sugar	50 mL

FILLING:

1	envelope unflavored gelatin	1
1/2 cup	lemon juice	125 mL
1 cup	granulated sugar	250 mL
1 tsp	grated lemon rind	5 mL
4	eggs, separated	4
1/4 cup	tequila	50 mL
2 tbsp	orange liqueur	25 mL

• **Crust:** In 10-inch (25 cm) pie plate, microwave butter at High for 40 to 50 seconds or until melted. Add pretzel crumbs and sugar; mix well. Press evenly over bottom and sides of pie plate. Microwave at High, uncovered, for 2 minutes. Set aside.

• **Filling:** In bowl, sprinkle gelatin over lemon juice. Let stand for 1 minute to soften. Stir in 1/2 cup (125 mL) of the sugar and lemon rind. Microwave at High for about 2 minutes or until mixture boils.

• In separate bowl, beat egg yolks. Gradually add hot liquid, mixing until smooth. Blend in tequila and orange liqueur. Refrigerate for about 30 minutes or until mixture is cold and slightly thickened; beat until smooth.

• Beat egg whites until frothy. Gradually add remaining sugar, beating until stiff peaks form. Gently fold into chilled mixture. Pour into prepared pie crust and chill until set, about 2 hours.

Margarita Pie

LEMON CURD PIE

Try this attractive and easy pie. Just prepare a simple crumb crust, microwave the smooth, thick yellow filling, add whipped cream, and you have a tart-sweet dessert. This pie is an excellent choice to follow fish dishes such as Salmon Ring with Hot Mayonnaise Sauce (recipe, p. 98).

3 tbsp	butter	50 mL
1 cup	gingersnap crumbs	250 mL
FILLING:		
3	eggs, beaten	3
1 cup	granulated sugar	250 mL
1/2 cup	lemon juice	125 mL
1/4 cup	butter, melted	50 mL
1 tbsp	grated lemon rind	15 mL
1 cup	whipping cream	250 mL

• In 9-inch (23 cm) pie plate, microwave butter at High for 30 seconds or until melted. Stir in crumbs until moistened; press against sides and bottom of pie plate to form crust. Microwave at High for 1-1/2 minutes or until set. Let cool completely.
• **Filling:** In 4-cup (1 L) measure, whisk together eggs and sugar until well combined; stir in lemon juice, butter and rind. Microwave at High for 3 to 5 minutes or until mixture boils and thickly coats spoon, stirring twice during cooking. Let cool; refrigerate until cold.
• Whip cream and fold half into cold lemon curd; spoon into prepared crust. Cover and refrigerate for at least 30 minutes or up to 8 hours. Just before serving, decoratively pipe reserved whipped cream over pie.

Vary the flavors of crumb crusts by using different cookies such as chocolate wafers or vanilla or spice-based cookies. Always use the amount of crumbs called for in the recipe.

BLACKENED BANANA BOATS

These whimsical Banana Boats are enhanced by the flavors of rum and orange. Make them the finishing touch to a menu that includes Ham and Leek Gratin (recipe, p. 65) and a spinach salad.

4	bananas (unpeeled)	4
3 tbsp	packed brown sugar	50 mL
3 tbsp	orange juice	50 mL
4 tsp	rum (optional)	20 mL
4 tsp	butter	20 mL
1/2 tsp	grated orange rind	2 mL
Pinch	cinnamon	Pinch

• With toothpick, pierce skins of bananas all over; place in 8-inch (2 L) square baking dish. Microwave at High for 4 to 5 minutes or until blackened all over; let cool slightly.
• Meanwhile, in small bowl, mix together brown sugar, orange juice, rum (if using), butter, orange rind and cinnamon; microwave at High for 1 minute or until butter has melted and sugar dissolved; stir.
• Transfer bananas to individual plates; slice through skin lengthwise. Spread skins apart slightly and press in ends to form boat shapes. Spoon 2 tbsp (25 mL) sauce into each banana; serve immediately. Makes 4 servings.

PEARS WITH ANISE

Anise adds a refreshing flavor to tender poached pears. (photo, p. 31)

4	pears, peeled, cored and sliced	4
3/4 cup	water	175 mL
1/2 cup	granulated sugar	125 mL
1 tsp	grated lemon rind	5 mL
1/2 tsp	aniseed	2 mL
	Whipped cream (optional)	

• In 6-cup (1.5 L) casserole, combine pears, water, sugar, lemon rind and aniseed; cover and microwave on High for 8 minutes or until pears are tender, stirring gently after 4 minutes. Refrigerate until serving time. Serve with whipped cream, if desired. Makes 4 servings.

POACHED PEARS

Here's a dessert that's always delicious and easy. Serve Poached Pears surrounded by yogurt, cream or a dessert sauce.(photo, p.161)

1 tbsp	lemon juice	15 mL
1/4 cup	water	50 mL
Pinch	each cinnamon and nutmeg	Pinch
2	large firm pears	2
Half	lemon	Half
	Chocolate Sauce (recipe, p. 161)	

• In 9-inch (23 cm) pie plate, combine lemon juice, water, cinnamon and nutmeg; set aside.
• Peel, halve and core pears; rub all over with lemon half. Arrange in pie plate cut side down in circle with thick ends toward outside. Cover with vented plastic wrap and microwave at High for 2 to 4 minutes or until pears are almost tender, rotating halfway through.
• Spoon poaching liquid over; cover and microwave at high for 1 to 2 minutes longer or until pears are just tender. Serve warm, at room temperature, or chilled with Chocolate Sauce. Makes 4 servings.

STUFFED BAKED APPLES

Serve this comforting easy-to-make dessert with whipped cream or ice cream. If you make it ahead of time, keep it covered until reheating. To reheat, microwave at High for 1 to 2 minutes or until warm.

4	apples	4
1/4 cup	packed brown sugar	50 mL
1 tbsp	finely chopped pecans	15 mL
1 tbsp	raisins	15 mL
2 tsp	butter	10 mL
1 tsp	cinnamon	5 mL
1 tsp	lemon juice	5 mL

• Remove core of each apple to 1/2 inch (1 cm) of bottom; prick skin all over. Place apples in 9-inch (23 cm) pie plate.
• In bowl, combine sugar, pecans, raisins, butter, cinnamon and lemon juice; spoon into apple cavities.
• Cover with vented plastic wrap and microwave at High for 7 to 9 minutes or until apples are tender, rotating halfway through. Makes 4 servings.

BLUEBERRY-PEACH CLAFOUTI

Strawberries or raspberries can be used in place of blueberries for a change of flavor. A 9-inch (23 cm) quiche dish or deep-dish pie plate will hold this dessert. (photo, p. 68)

1/3 cup	granulated sugar	75 mL
4	peaches, peeled and cut in thin wedges	4
1 cup	fresh or frozen blueberries	250 mL
1/2 lb	cream cheese, cut in cubes	250 g
2 tbsp	all-purpose flour	25 mL
1	egg	1
1	egg yolk	1
2 tbsp	whipping cream	25 mL
1 tsp	vanilla	5 mL

• Sprinkle greased 10-inch (25 cm) pie plate with 2 tbsp (25 mL) of the sugar. Arrange peaches like spokes of a wheel on plate; scatter blueberries among peaches.
• In food processor, combine cream cheese, flour, egg, egg yolk, cream, vanilla and remaining sugar; process until smooth. Pour over fruit.
• Microwave at Medium (50%) for 10 to 12 minutes or until barely set, rotating halfway through. Let stand until consistency of soft custard, at least 10 minutes. Serve warm or chilled. Makes about 4 servings.

Lemon Floating Islands

LEMON FLOATING ISLANDS

Fast and fresh, this citrus version of a classic dessert is cooked in less than 10 minutes in the microwave oven.

1-1/2 cups	orange juice	375 mL
1 tbsp	lemon juice	15 mL
2 tbsp	cornstarch	25 mL
2 tbsp	honey	25 mL
1	stick cinnamon, about 2 inches (5 cm)	1
2	egg whites	2
1/4 tsp	cream of tartar	1 mL
3 tbsp	granulated sugar	50 mL
1 tsp	grated orange rind	5 mL

• In 4-cup (1 L) glass measure, combine orange and lemon juices, cornstarch, honey and cinnamon stick; microwave at High, uncovered, for 4-1/2 to 5-1/2 minutes or until mixture boils, stirring once. Pour into shallow 6-cup (1.5 L) microwaveable serving dish; remove cinnamon stick.

• Beat egg whites with cream of tartar until frothy. Gradually beat in sugar until stiff peaks form. Spoon 4 separate mounds of meringue onto orange sauce; sprinkle with orange rind. Microwave at High, uncovered, for 1-1/2 to 2 minutes or until meringue is set. Serve warm or cool. Makes 4 servings.

CHOCOLATE MOCHA PUDDING

Creamy and smooth, you can make this dessert up to a day ahead and refrigerate it until serving time. Just before serving, garnish with fresh berries or sliced bananas.

1/2 cup	granulated sugar	125 mL
3 tbsp	unsweetened cocoa powder, sifted	50 mL
3 tbsp	cornstarch	50 mL
1/2 tsp	cinnamon	2 mL
1/4 tsp	instant coffee granules	1 mL
2 cups	milk	500 mL
1 tbsp	butter	15 mL
1 tsp	vanilla	5 mL

• In 8-cup (2 L) bowl, combine sugar, cocoa, cornstarch, cinnamon and coffee granules; blend until smooth. Gradually stir in milk. Microwave at High for 5 to 6 minutes or until pudding starts to come to boil and has thickened slightly, whisking every 2 minutes. Stir in butter and vanilla. Place waxed paper or plastic wrap directly on pudding surface. Refrigerate until serving time, at least 2 hours.

• Remove wrap and whisk gently; spoon into individual dessert dishes. Makes 4 servings.

Stirring is important when making cornstarch-thickened puddings in a microwave oven. To prevent the thickener from settling to the bottom in a mass, stir well after one-third of the cooking time and again after two-thirds; stir once more after cooking is completed.

FRESH BERRY TRIFLE
Line the bottom and sides of a 6-cup (1.5 L) glass serving bowl with jelly roll slices or lady fingers. Sprinkle with 2 tbsp (25 mL) sherry, if desired. Pour half of cooled Rich Vanilla Pudding over top. Spoon on 1-1/2 cups (375 mL) fresh berries. Cover with remaining pudding; chill.

At serving time, garnish with a piping of whipped cream and a few fresh berries. Makes 4 to 6 servings.

Fresh Berry Trifle

RICH VANILLA PUDDING

This quick and easy pudding is perfect to use in a trifle or to pour over sliced bananas or fresh berries as a simple-supper dessert.

3 cups	milk	750 mL
3/4 cup	granulated sugar	175 mL
1/4 cup	cornstarch	50 mL
3	egg yolks, beaten	3
2 tbsp	butter	25 mL
1 tsp	vanilla	5 mL

• In large bowl, combine milk, sugar and cornstarch; microwave at High, uncovered, for 8 minutes or until slightly thickened, stirring every 2 minutes. Microwave at High for 1 minute longer, stirring twice.
• Whisk about one-third of the hot mixture into egg yolks; return egg yolk mixture to bowl and microwave at High for about 2 minutes or until bubbly around edge.
• Add butter and vanilla; stir until butter has melted. Place plastic wrap directly on surface. Refrigerate until serving time, at least 2 hours. Makes about 3 cups (750 mL).

CREAMY RICE PUDDING

Since microwave ovens can have different cooking patterns, move these individual dishes several times during cooking. Remove each one as it sets – don't wait until they are all cooked to remove them.

1/4 lb	cream cheese	125 g
3	eggs	3
3/4 cup	milk	175 mL
1/2 cup	granulated sugar	125 mL
1/2 cup	cooked rice	125 mL
1/2 cup	raisins	125 mL
1 tsp	lemon rind	5 mL
1/4 tsp	cinnamon	1 mL
1/4 tsp	nutmeg	1 mL

• In 8-cup (2 L) measure, microwave cream cheese at High for 30 seconds or until softened; whisk until smooth.
• Gradually stir in eggs, milk, sugar, rice, raisins, lemon rind, cinnamon and nutmeg.
• Pour into four 1-cup (250 mL) dessert dishes and arrange in circle in oven. Microwave at Medium (50%) for 8 to 12 minutes or until edges and centers are thickened but not set, rotating dishes a quarter turn every 3 minutes and removing as done.
• Let stand for 15 minutes. Serve warm or chilled. Makes 4 servings.

CRÈME CARAMEL

A classic dessert that is simple to make in the microwave oven.

1/2 cup	granulated sugar	125 mL
3 tbsp	water	50 mL
CUSTARD:		
2 cups	milk	500 mL
4	eggs	4
1/4 cup	granulated sugar	50 mL
1 tsp	vanilla	5 mL

• In 2-cup (500 mL) measure, combine sugar and water; microwave, uncovered, at High for 4 to 6 minutes or until golden. Pour into 6 lightly greased 3/4-cup (175 mL) custard cups; set aside.
• **Custard:** In 4-cup (1 L) measure, microwave milk, uncovered, at High for 4 to 6 minutes or until scalded and bubbles appear around edge.
• In bowl, beat together eggs, sugar and vanilla; whisk in scalded milk and pour evenly into custard cups. Cover with waxed paper and microwave at Medium (50%) for 6 to 8 minutes or until knife inserted near center comes out clean, rearranging cups every 2 minutes. Let stand on counter until cool; refrigerate for 1 hour or until chilled.
• To serve, loosen around edge of custard with sharp knife; invert onto plate. Makes 6 servings.

INDIVIDUAL COCONUT FLANS

Here's a pleasant change from plain custard. Use frozen orange juice concentrate instead of rum, if desired.

1 cup	milk	250 mL
1	can (7 oz/207 mL) sweetened cream of coconut	1
3	eggs	3
2	egg yolks	2
1 tbsp	cornstarch	15 mL
1 tbsp	rum	15 mL
2 tbsp	packed brown sugar	25 mL

• In 2-cup (500 mL) measure, microwave milk at High for about 1-1/2 minutes or until steaming.
• In food processor or blender, combine cream of coconut, eggs, egg yolks, cornstarch and rum; process until smooth. With motor running, gradually add hot milk through feed tube.
• Place 1 tsp (5 mL) brown sugar in each of six 3/4-cup (175 mL) custard cups. Divide custard among cups. Cover with waxed paper and microwave at Medium (50%) for 7 to 10 minutes or until almost firm and knife inserted in centers comes out clean, rotating dishes every 2 minutes. Let stand until cool; cover and refrigerate until chilled. Makes 6 servings.

PEAR AND CRANBERRY CRISP

Fast, light and tangy, this is a traditional version of a wonderful comfort food. For a modern version, substitute 100% Bran cereal or All Bran for the flour in the topping. Variations for using other fruits in season are given below.

4	pears, peeled, cored and sliced	4
2 cups	cranberries, fresh or frozen	500 mL
2/3 cup	packed brown sugar	150 mL
1/2 cup	rolled oats	125 mL
1/2 cup	all-purpose flour	125 mL
1 tsp	cinnamon	5 mL
1/4 cup	butter, softened	50 mL

• In 8-cup (2 L) shallow baking dish, toss pears with cranberries. Mix together sugar, rolled oats, flour and cinnamon. With pastry blender or fingertips, work in butter. (If using bran cereal, break up slightly when blending in butter.) Sprinkle over fruit, pressing down lightly and evenly.
• Microwave, uncovered, at High for 4 minutes; rotate dish. Microwave at High for 3 to 4 minutes or until fruit is fork-tender and topping is slightly browned. Let stand for 5 minutes. Makes 4 servings.

TO MAKE 2 SERVINGS:

• In 6-cup (1.5 L) shallow baking dish, toss 2 pears (peeled, cored and sliced) with 1 cup (250 mL) cranberries. Mix together 1/3 cup (75 mL) brown sugar, 1/3 cup (75 mL) rolled oats, 1/3 cup (75 mL) flour and 1/2 tsp (2 mL) cinnamon. With pastry blender or fingertips, work in 2 tbsp (25 mL) butter. Sprinkle over fruit, pressing down lightly and evenly.
• Microwave, uncovered, at High for 3 minutes; rotate dish. Microwave at High for 2 to 3 minutes or until fruit is fork-tender and topping is slightly browned. Let stand for 5 minutes.

VARIATIONS:

PEACH AND BLUEBERRY CRISP:

• Substitute 4 cups (1 L) sliced, peeled peaches or nectarines and 1 cup (250 mL) blueberries for the pears and cranberries.

APPLE AND RAISIN CRISP:

• Substitute 6 cups (1.5 L) sliced, peeled apples (about 4 large) and 1/2 cup (125 mL) raisins for the pears and cranberries.

FRESH PLUM CRISP:

• Substitute 4 cups (1 L) quartered or sliced plums for the pears. Omit the cranberries.

(Clockwise from top) Pear and Cranberry Crisp; Peach and Blueberry Crisp; Fresh Plum Crisp

FRUIT CRISP TIP
If making the crisp with frozen peaches or plums, the fruit needs only enough thawing to break slices apart. If making the crisp ahead of time with these frozen fruits, the fruit layers will become very juicy while standing. To compensate, toss fruit with 2 tsp (10 mL) cornstarch before cooking.

MINI-MANDARIN CHEESECAKES

Individual cheesecakes are topped with mandarin orange sections to make a light, creamy dessert.

1	can (10 oz/284 mL) mandarin oranges	1
6	vanilla wafers	6
1/2 lb	cream cheese	250 g
1/3 cup	granulated sugar	75 mL
1	egg	1
1/2 tsp	vanilla	2 mL

• Drain oranges, reserving 1 tsp (5 mL) juice; set aside. Line six 3/4-cup (175 mL) custard cups with large paper baking cups. Place 1 vanilla wafer in each, flat side down.

• In bowl, microwave cream cheese at Medium-Low (30%) for 1 minute or until slightly softened. Beat in sugar, egg, vanilla and reserved orange juice until well blended. Place 2 tbsp (25 mL) in each custard cup; top each with 4 orange sections. Divide remaining mixture evenly among cups.

• Arrange cups in circle in microwave. Microwave at Medium-Low (30%) for 13 to 15 minutes or until set and no longer sticky when touched lightly, rearranging cups twice. Let stand on flat surface for 10 minutes. Refrigerate for at least 30 minutes or up to 1 day. Garnish with remaining orange sections. Makes 6 servings.

Sauces, Spreads and Sweets

A delicious sauce often makes the difference between an ordinary meal and an exciting one. Making superb sauces no longer has to be a time-consuming chore. The Easy Tomato Sauce (p. 28) is perfect over pasta or meat and the quick and easy Cucumber Sauce (p. 159) makes fish sticks really special. Try our Basic White Sauce (p. 159), for example, with its variations. Sweet toppings are easy, too, from an Orange Custard Sauce (p. 160) made without constant stirring to a sinfully rich Chocolate Sauce (p. 161). Relishes, chutneys, spreads and candies can also be made in less time than ever before.

SPAGHETTI SAUCE WITH MEAT

Full of vegetables, this basic spaghetti sauce is thick and hearty.

1/3 cup	each chopped onion, carrot and celery	75 mL
1 tbsp	olive oil	15 mL
1	clove garlic, minced	1
3/4 lb	lean ground beef	375 g
1	can (19 oz/540 mL) tomatoes (undrained), chopped	1
1/4 cup	tomato paste	50 mL
1 tsp	dried basil	5 mL
1/2 tsp	dried oregano	2 mL
Pinch	hot pepper flakes (optional)	Pinch
	Salt and pepper	

• In 8-cup (2 L) measuring cup or casserole, combine onion, carrot, celery, oil and garlic; cover with vented plastic wrap or lid and microwave at High for 3 to 5 minutes or until vegetables are tender-crisp, stirring once.
• Stir in beef; cover and microwave at High for about 5 minutes or until meat is no longer pink, stirring once to break up meat. Drain any fat from dish.
• Stir in tomatoes, tomato paste, basil, oregano, and hot pepper flakes (if using); cover and microwave at High for 10 to 15 minutes or until sauce has thickened, stirring twice. Season with salt and pepper to taste. Makes about 4 cups (1 L).

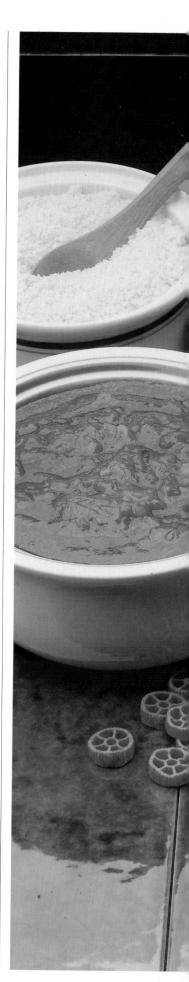

(Clockwise from bottom) Clam and Mushroom Sauce (p. 29); Easy Tomato Sauce (p. 28); Spaghetti Sauce with Meat

*Microwave Blender
Hollandaise*

MICROWAVE BLENDER HOLLANDAISE

*Now you can make Hollandaise sauce with
the help of your blender and microwave oven.
Follow the directions and you'll be thrilled
at how smooth, creamy and easy it is.*

3	egg yolks	3
4 tsp	lemon juice	20 mL
Dash	hot pepper sauce	Dash
Pinch	each salt and pepper	Pinch
2/3 cup	butter	150 mL

• In blender, combine egg yolks, lemon juice,
hot pepper sauce, salt and pepper; process
until well blended.
• In 2-cup (250 mL) measure, cover butter
with vented plastic wrap and microwave at
High for about 2 minutes or just until melted
and barely bubbling around edge.
• With blender running, gradually add hot
butter in slow steady stream; blend for
30 seconds. Taste and adjust seasoning if
necessary. (Hollandaise can be covered and
kept warm for up to 2 hours by standing
container in very hot tap water.) At serving
time, if necessary, reheat at Medium (50%)
for 1/2 to 1 minute, stirring every 15 seconds.
Makes about 1 cup (250 mL) sauce.

BASIC WHITE SAUCE

No more lumpy sauces once you learn to mix them in the microwave. Try the variations given below.

1/4 cup	butter	50 mL
1/4 cup	all-purpose flour	50 mL
2 cups	milk	500 mL
	Salt, pepper and nutmeg	

- In 4-cup measure, microwave butter at High for 45 to 55 seconds or until melted. Stir in flour to form smooth paste. Gradually whisk in milk.
- Microwave at High for 5 to 7 minutes or until boiling and thickened, whisking after 2 minutes then every minute. Season with salt, pepper and nutmeg to taste. Makes about 2-1/4 cups (550 mL).

VARIATIONS:

CHEESE SAUCE:

- Stir 1 tsp (5 mL) dry mustard or 1 tbsp (15 mL) Dijon mustard and 2 cups (500 mL) shredded Cheddar cheese into Basic White Sauce at end of cooking time. Microwave at High for 1 minute or until cheese has melted; stir. Makes about 2-2/3 cups (650 mL).

MUSHROOM HERB SAUCE:

- Use 6-cup (1.5 L) measure or bowl. Stir 2 cups (500 mL) sliced mushrooms, 2 tbsp (25 mL) chopped green onions and 1/2 tsp (2 mL) dried tarragon into the melted butter. Microwave at High for 2 to 3 minutes or until mushrooms are softened. Stir in flour and continue with recipe for Basic White Sauce. Makes about 3 cups (750 mL).

• Change the flavor of the Cheese Sauce by using different cheeses such as Swiss, Muenster or processed.
• Fresh savory, thyme, rosemary or basil may be used in place of tarragon in the Mushroom Herb Sauce. To substitute fresh herbs for dried, use three times the amount.

CUCUMBER SAUCE

This quick and easy sauce is delicious served with fish – particularly Homemade Fish Sticks (recipe, p. 96).

1	small cucumber	1
1/4 cup	mayonnaise	50 mL
1/4 cup	plain yogurt	50 mL
1 tbsp	finely chopped fresh parsley (or 1 tsp/5 mL dried)	15 mL
2 tsp	lemon juice	10 mL
1 tsp	finely chopped onion	5 mL

- Peel cucumber (if bitter) and scoop out seeds; grate coarsely to make 3/4 cup (175 mL).
- In 2-cup (500 mL) measure, combine cucumber, mayonnaise, yogurt, parsley, lemon juice and onion. Microwave at High for 2 to 3 minutes or until warm, stirring once. Makes about 1-1/4 cups (300 mL).

LEMON SAUCE

This light zesty sauce is delicious served over cottage pudding or hot Gingerbread (recipe, p. 138).

2 tbsp	butter	25 mL
1/2 cup	granulated sugar	125 mL
2 tbsp	cornstarch	25 mL
1 cup	water	250 mL
1 tsp	grated lemon rind	5 mL
1/4 cup	lemon juice	50 mL

- In 4-cup (1 L) measure, microwave butter at High for 15 to 30 seconds or until melted.
- Mix together sugar and cornstarch; add to melted butter along with water, lemon rind and juice. Microwave at High for 3 to 4 minutes or until boiling and thickened, stirring twice. Makes 1-1/2 cups (375 mL).

CRANBERRY SAUCE

You can substitute 1/2 tsp (2 mL) almond extract for the amaretto in this recipe, or use orange juice instead of the water.

2 cups	cranberries	500 mL
1/2 cup	granulated sugar	125 mL
2 tbsp	water	25 mL
1 tbsp	amaretto	15 mL

• In 4-cup (1 L) measure, combine cranberries, sugar, water and amaretto. Microwave at High for 6 to 8 minutes. Let stand, covered, for 5 minutes. Chill before serving. Makes about 1-1/2 cups (375 mL).

ORANGE CUSTARD SAUCE

Cooking this sauce in the microwave eliminates the constant stirring usually required when cooked on the stove top. Serve with your favorite fresh fruit.

1 cup	milk	250 mL
3 tbsp	granulated sugar	50 mL
4 tsp	cornstarch	20 mL
2	egg yolks	2
1 tbsp	grated orange rind	15 mL
1/4 cup	orange juice	50 mL
1 tbsp	orange liqueur (optional)	15 mL
1 tsp	vanilla	5 mL

• In 4-cup (1 L) measure, whisk together 1/4 cup (50 mL) of the milk, sugar, cornstarch and egg yolks; set aside.
• In 2-cup (500 mL) measure, microwave remaining milk at High for 2 minutes or until boiling; gradually pour into egg yolk mixture, whisking constantly. Stir in orange rind and juice; microwave at High for 2 minutes or until thickened, stirring twice. Blend in liqueur (if using) and vanilla.
• Cover and refrigerate for about 1 hour or until chilled, or for up to 2 days. Makes 1-1/2 cups (375 mL).

RHUBARB-STRAWBERRY SAUCE

Delicious simply served over pound cake or ice cream, you can turn this sauce into an easy yet elegant dessert by layering it with plain yogurt in parfait dishes or folding in whipped cream to make a creamy compôte.

4 cups	frozen rhubarb pieces (about 1 lb/ 500 g)	1 L
1/4 cup	granulated sugar	50 mL
1/4 cup	frozen strawberry juice concentrate, thawed	50 mL
1 tsp	cornstarch	5 mL
1/2 tsp	grated orange rind	2 mL

• In 6-cup (1.5 L) dish, sprinkle rhubarb with sugar. Mix together strawberry concentrate, cornstarch and orange rind; pour over rhubarb mixture and stir to coat evenly.
• Cover with vented plastic wrap and microwave at High for 7 to 9 minutes or until rhubarb is tender and sauce has thickened, gently stirring once. Let cool. Serve at room temperature or chilled. Makes about 2 cups (500 mL).

Chocolate Sauce over Poached Pears (p. 150)

CHOCOLATE SAUCE

This sauce is sinfully good over ice cream or Poached Pears (recipe, p. 150) or spooned onto cream puffs or pound cake.

1/3 cup	granulated sugar	75 mL
1/4 cup	unsweetened cocoa powder	50 mL
1/4 tsp	cinnamon	1 mL
3 tbsp	light cream	50 mL
1 tbsp	corn syrup	15 mL
1/4 cup	butter	50 mL
1/2 tsp	vanilla	2 mL
	Ice cream	

• In 4-cup (1 L) measure or bowl, combine sugar, cocoa and cinnamon. Stir in cream and corn syrup; blend well. Microwave at High for 2 minutes or until simmering; stir in butter until melted. Blend in vanilla. Serve warm or at room temperature over ice cream. (Sauce can be covered and refrigerated for up to 2 weeks.) Makes 3/4 cup (175 mL).

ZUCCHINI AND PEPPER RELISH

This quick relish is perfect for hot dogs and hamburgers or to serve with a cold meat platter. The recipe yields slightly more than three 1-cup (250 mL) jars so prepare four jars just in case.

4 cups	finely chopped zucchini (about 1-1/2 lb/750 g)	1 L
1 cup	finely chopped onions	250 mL
1/2 cup	finely chopped sweet red pepper	125 mL
2 tbsp	pickling salt	25 mL
1-1/4 cups	granulated sugar	300 mL
1/2 cup	white vinegar	125 mL
1/2 tsp	dry mustard	2 mL
1/2 tsp	celery seed	2 mL
1/4 tsp	pepper	1 mL
1/4 tsp	turmeric	1 mL
1 tsp	cornstarch	5 mL
2 tsp	cold water	10 mL

• In 12-cup (3 L) bowl, combine zucchini, onions and red pepper; sprinkle with salt and stir to mix. Let stand for 1 to 2 hours, stirring occasionally. Drain and rinse thoroughly under cold running water; drain again, pressing out excess moisture.
• In 12-cup (3 L) bowl, combine sugar, vinegar, mustard, celery seed, pepper and turmeric. Cover with vented plastic wrap and microwave at High for 3 minutes or until mixture comes to boil, stirring once.
• Add drained vegetables and microwave, covered, at High for 3 to 4 minutes or until mixture boils; stir well. Microwave at High, covered, for 3 to 5 minutes longer, stirring twice, or until vegetables are tender.
• Blend together cornstarch and cold water; stir into relish. Microwave at High, covered, for 1 minute or until mixture is thickened slightly.
• Pour relish into prepared jars, leaving 1/8-inch (3 mm) headspace. Immediately seal with mason-type lids and let cool; wipe and label. Store in cool, dark, dry place. Makes about three 1-cup (250 mL) jars.

APRICOT SPREAD

Delicious on toast or hot biscuits, this spread can also be used as a filling for tarts, or as a rich cake or jelly roll filling. It keeps well in the refrigerator for 3 to 4 weeks.

1 cup	chopped dried apricots	250 mL
3/4 cup	(approx) water	175 mL
1-1/2 cups	granulated sugar	375 mL
3	egg yolks	3
1/2 cup	butter, cut in chunks	125 mL
1 tsp	grated lemon rind	5 mL
2 tsp	lemon juice	10 mL
1 tbsp	orange or citrus-flavored liqueur (optional)	15 mL

• In 8-cup (2 L) measure, microwave apricots and water at High for 5 minutes or until apricots are tender and most of the liquid is absorbed, stirring twice. Watch carefully that apricots do not dry and burn, adding 2 to 3 tbsp (25 to 50 mL) more water if necessary. Transfer to blender or food processor and blend until smooth; set aside.
• In bowl, lightly beat together sugar and egg yolks; add butter, lemon rind and juice along with puréed apricots. Microwave at Medium (50%), covered, for 5 to 6 minutes or until thickened and slightly bubbly around edge of bowl, stirring several times.
• Stir in liqueur (if using). Pour into hot sterilized jars; seal at once with paraffin or mason-type lids. Refrigerate for up to 4 weeks. Makes about 2-3/4 cups (675 mL).

STERILIZING AND SEALING JARS
Wash jars in hot soapy water; rinse well and set on metal tray. About 20 minutes before the preserve is ready, set tray in 225°F (110°C) oven for 15 minutes, then turn off heat and leave in oven until needed.

Fill sterilized jars, leaving 1/2-inch (1 cm) headspace if jars are to be sealed with paraffin, 1/8-inch (3 mm) headspace if using mason-type jars with new lids that have sealing compound on them.

To seal with paraffin, pour thin layer of melted paraffin* over surface of preserve, tilting and rotating each jar to extend seal to rim. Let jars cool completely, then apply a second thin layer of paraffin. To seal mason-type jars, boil lids for 5 minutes. As soon as jars are filled, cover with lids and seal with bands.
* Paraffin will not melt in a microwave oven. It should be melted carefully over hot water.

QUICK FRUIT CHUTNEY

*Chutney is delicious with curries or cold meats.
Now you can cook it in ten minutes so you'll
always have some on hand.*

1 cup	chopped mixed dried fruits	250 mL
1/3 cup	cider vinegar	75 mL
1/3 cup	orange juice	75 mL
1/4 cup	raisins	50 mL
3 tbsp	packed brown sugar	50 mL
1-1/2 tsp	finely chopped gingerroot	7 mL
1/2 tsp	crushed coriander seeds	2 mL
1/4 tsp	salt	1 mL
Pinch	each ground cloves, cayenne and black pepper	Pinch

• In 4-cup (1 L) measure, combine chopped
dried fruits, vinegar, orange juice, raisins,
sugar, gingerroot, coriander seeds, salt,
cloves, cayenne and black pepper.
• Cover with vented plastic wrap and
microwave at High for 7 to 10 minutes or
until fruits are tender and liquid absorbed,
stirring twice. Makes about 1 cup (250 mL).

**SETTING POINT
FOR JAM**
*Use the plate or wrinkle
test. Place two small
plates in freezer to
chill before you begin
making jam. As setting
time approaches,
remove measure from
microwave, drop about
1/2 tsp (2 mL) jam onto
plate and let cool for
1 minute. Run your
fingertip through jam
on plate; if surface
wrinkles, setting point
has been reached. If
sample remains syrupy,
return measure to the
microwave and continue
cooking, repeating test
with other chilled plate.
Repeat test every 30
seconds, using colder
plate.*

PLUM JAM

*This recipe makes a true mini-batch, small
enough to make in an 8-cup (2 L) measure.
This jam can also be made in a microwaveable
casserole, but the measuring cup has a spout
for easy pouring and a handle that stays cool.*

6	large plums (about 1 lb/500 g)	6
1-1/2 cups	granulated sugar	375 mL
1 tbsp	lemon juice	15 mL
1 tsp	finely grated orange rind	5 mL

• Pit plums. In food processor, process with
on-and-off motion until finely chopped. (You
should have 2 cups/500 mL.) Transfer to
8-cup (2 L) measure; blend in sugar, juice
and rind. Microwave, uncovered, at High
for 6 minutes; stir. Microwave at High for
10 to 15 minutes longer, stirring every
3 minutes, or until jam thickens and sets (see
sidebar, this page).
• Pour jam into hot sterilized jars, leaving
1/2-inch (1 cm) headspace. Seal with paraffin
or mason-type lids and store in cool, dark,
dry place. Makes two 1-cup (250 mL) jars.

STRAWBERRY SPREAD

*This is tasty as either a jam-like spread or as
a sauce for ice cream. Since fruit varies so
much in ripeness, the results with this spread
will vary with each batch made. Substitute
raspberries or blackberries for the strawberries
but watch carefully because the cooking time
needed to reach setting point varies for each.*

4 cups	frozen whole strawberries	1 L
1-1/2 cups	granulated sugar	375 mL
1 tbsp	lemon juice	15 mL

• In large measure or bowl (at least 8 cups/
2 L), combine strawberries, sugar and lemon
juice; microwave at High for about 3 to 4
minutes until berries are defrosted and sugar
has dissolved, stirring twice.
• Mash gently with potato masher; microwave
at High for about 6 minutes or until mixture
comes to boil, stirring several times.
Microwave, uncovered, at High for
16 minutes, stirring every 4 minutes.
Microwave for 2 to 8 minutes longer or until
setting point (see sidebar, this page) is
reached, stirring every minute.
• Pour into hot sterilized jars; seal at once
with paraffin or mason-type lids. Makes about
2 cups (500 mL).

CHOCOLATE FUDGE

This all-time favorite treat has nuts and coconut added for that extra-special zing. Kids and teens will whip it up in a jiffy – and eat it just as quickly!

4 cups	sifted icing sugar	1 L
3/4 cup	unsweetened cocoa powder, sifted	175 mL
1/4 cup	milk	50 mL
1/2 cup	butter	125 mL
1/3 cup	shredded coconut	75 mL
1/3 cup	chopped nuts	75 mL
1 tsp	vanilla	5 mL

• In large bowl, combine icing sugar and cocoa; pour in milk but do not stir. Place butter on top. Microwave at High for 2 to 4 minutes or until butter is melted and bubbling, rotating twice. Add coconut, nuts and vanilla; stir to mix completely.
• Pour into well-greased 9- x 5-inch (2 L) loaf pan; refrigerate for 2 to 3 hours or until firm. Makes about 1-1/4 lb (625 g).

GRANOLA

You can add 1/4 cup (50 mL) sesame seeds before cooking or 1/2 cup (125 mL) chopped dates, dried apricots or dried mixed fruit along with, or instead of, the raisins.

3 cups	rolled oats	750 mL
1/2 cup	wheat germ	125 mL
1/2 cup	flaked coconut	125 mL
1/2 cup	toasted chopped almonds*	125 mL
1/3 cup	shelled sunflower seeds	75 mL
1/4 cup	packed dark brown sugar	50 mL
1/4 cup	honey	50 mL
1/4 cup	vegetable oil	50 mL
1/2 tsp	vanilla	2 mL
1/2 cup	raisins	125 mL

• In 8-cup (2 L) bowl, stir together rolled oats, wheat germ, coconut, almonds, sunflower seeds and sugar.
• Mix together honey, oil and vanilla; stir into dry mixture and mix until completely moistened. Microwave at High for 6 to 8 minutes or until toasted, stirring twice.
• Add raisins and toss to mix; spread on foil-lined baking sheet and let cool completely. Break up clumps; store in airtight container. Makes about 6 cups (1.5 L).

*To toast almonds, spread in pie plate and microwave at High for 5 to 7 minutes or until toasted, stirring every minute.

ALMOND BRITTLE

Tempting and crunchy, you'll find it hard to have just one piece. Leave the brown skins on the almonds or use blanched almonds.

1-1/2 cups	granulated sugar	375 mL
1/2 cup	corn syrup	125 mL
1/2 cup	water	125 mL
2 cups	almonds	500 mL
1 tbsp	butter	15 mL
1 tsp	baking soda	5 mL
1 tsp	vanilla	5 mL

• In 8-cup (2 L) measure, combine sugar, corn syrup, water and almonds; microwave at High, uncovered, for 13 minutes. Microwave at High for 30 to 90 seconds longer or until hard-crack stage (candy thermometer registers 300°F/150°C), checking every 30 seconds.
• Add butter, baking soda and vanilla; stir to mix.
• Pour onto greased baking sheet and let cool. Break into pieces and store in air-tight container.

(Left to right) Chocolate Fudge; Granola; Orange-Glazed Nuts; Almond Brittle

ORANGE-GLAZED NUTS

Use almonds, mixed nuts or pecans instead of walnut halves for a change of flavor.

2 cups	walnut halves	500 mL
1 tbsp	grated orange rind	15 mL
2 tbsp	orange juice	25 mL
1/4 cup	packed brown sugar	50 mL
1 tsp	cinnamon	5 mL

• In well-buttered pie plate, combine walnuts, orange rind and juice; stir to coat nuts well.
• Mix together brown sugar and cinnamon; sprinkle over nuts and stir to coat. Microwave at High, uncovered, for 5 to 7 minutes or until nuts are heated through and glazed.
• Let cool for 5 minutes. Transfer nuts to baking sheet, spreading out to cool completely. Makes 2 cups (500 mL).

A Microwave Cooking Reference Guide

In this section, we've provided useful charts and directions to give you a handy reference guide at your fingertips. You'll find information on cooking fresh and frozen vegetables (p. 168), defrosting and cooking meat, poultry and fish (p. 170), as well as reheating foods (p. 172). With the help of the Microwave Shortcuts (p. 173), you can make the most of this versatile appliance. There's even a test for determining the wattage of your microwave oven (p. 172).

COOKING CHART FOR FRESH VEGETABLES

VEGETABLE	QUANTITY	WATER	PREPARATION	MINUTES COOKING TIME	MINUTES STANDING TIME
Artichokes	2 medium	1/4 cup (50 mL)	Wash; trim stem. Cut 1 inch (2.5 cm) off tops; snip tips from each leaf. Brush with lemon juice. Place upside down in dish; cover with vented plastic wrap.	8-12; rotate once	5
Asparagus	1 lb (500 g)	2 tbsp (25 mL)	Wash; snip off tough ends. Arrange with tips in center of dish. Cover with vented plastic wrap.	6-8; rotate once	5
Beans, green or wax	1 lb (500 g) 3 cups (750 mL)	1/4 cup (50 mL)	Wash; trim. Cut into 1-1/2-inch (4 cm) pieces. Cover with vented plastic wrap.	7-10; stir once	5
Beets, whole	4 medium	1/4 cup (50 mL)	Do not peel. Leave at least 1 inch (2.5 cm) stem. Cover with vented plastic wrap.	12-15; rotate twice	5
Broccoli	1 lb (500 g)	2 tbsp (25 mL)	Wash; trim. Shake off excess water. Place stems towards outside of dish. Cover with vented plastic wrap.	6-9; rotate once	3
Brussels Sprouts	1 lb (500 g)	2 tbsp (25 mL)	Cover with vented plastic wrap.	6-8; stir once	5
Cabbage	1 lb (500 g) (small head)	2 tbsp (25 mL)	Cut in 6 wedges. Cover with vented plastic wrap.	6-9; rotate once	3
Carrots, sliced	2 cups (500 mL)	2 tbsp (25 mL)	Cover with vented plastic wrap.	6-8; stir once	5
Carrots, small whole	3/4 lb (375 g)	2 tbsp (25 mL)	Cover with vented plastic wrap.	6-8; stir once	5
Cauliflower, florets	3 cups (750 mL)	2 tbsp (25 mL)	Cover with vented plastic wrap.	6-8; stir once	5
Corn-on-the-cob	2 ears	——	Remove silk and leave in husks tied with string, or husk and wrap in plastic wrap. Place on paper towel.	4-6; rotate once or rearrange	5
	4 ears			7-10; rotate once or rearrange	5
Parsnips, peeled and sliced	3 cups (750 mL)	2 tbsp (25 mL)	Cover with vented plastic wrap.	6-8; stir once	5
Peas, green	2 cups (500 mL) shelled	2 tbsp (25 mL)	Cover with vented plastic wrap.	5-7; stir once	5

VEGETABLE	QUANTITY	WATER	PREPARATION	MINUTES COOKING TIME	MINUTES STANDING TIME
Potatoes To micro-bake with skin on:	2 large	——	Prick with fork. Place on paper towel.	6-8; turn or rearrange once	5 wrapped in terry towel or paper towel
	4 large		Same as above	13-16; turn or rearrange once	Same as above
To cook, peeled and quartered:	4 cups (1 L)	2 tbsp (25 mL)	Cover with vented plastic wrap.	12-15; stir once	5
Rutabaga, peeled and cubed	3 cups (750 mL)	2 tbsp (25 mL)	Cover with vented plastic wrap.	7-9; stir once	5
Spinach	4 cups (1 L)	——	Wash; remove tough stems. Cover with vented plastic wrap.	4-5	5
Squash, peeled and cubed	3 cups (750 mL)	——	Cover with vented plastic wrap.	7-9; stir once	5
Sweet potatoes, small	same as potatoes				

COOKING CHART FOR FROZEN VEGETABLES

VEGETABLE	QUANTITY	MICROWAVE COOKING TIME	QUICK SEASONING ADDITIONS
Asparagus	2 pkg (each 300 g)	9 min.	Butter; lemon.
Broccoli	3 cups (750 mL) chopped	7 min.	Cheese sauce; sautéed sliced onions and water chestnuts; soy sauce; chopped walnuts; slivered almonds.
Brussels Sprouts	4 cups (1 L)	8 min.	Lemon juice; wine vinegar; chopped chives; minced garlic; paprika.
Carrots	3 cups (750 mL) sliced	9 min.	Chopped parsley, rosemary, cumin, dill; chopped walnuts or pecans.
Corn	2 cups (500 mL)	5 min.	Bacon bits; chopped sweet red and green peppers.
Lima Beans	2 cups (500 mL)	7 min.	Chopped parsley; diced onion or tomatoes; mustard; paprika.
Peas	2 cups (500 mL)	5 min.	Chopped parsley, dill or mint; sautéed sliced green onions, celery or mushrooms.
Rutabaga	3 cups (750 mL) cubed	8 min.	Butter.
Squash	3 cups (750 mL) cubed	6 min.	Lemon and brown sugar; maple syrup.

• *Microwave vegetables, covered with lid or plastic wrap, at High as directed in chart. Let stand, covered, for 2 minutes. Drain and add Quick Seasoning Additions, if desired.*

DEFROSTING GUIDE
FOR MEAT, POULTRY & FISH

• Remove food from wrapping or heat will build up inside packaging and start to cook the outside before inside has thawed. Place on rack to allow juices to drain.
• Halfway through defrosting time, separate individual pieces or break up ground meats, arranging icier pieces toward outside of dish. Turn over large cuts. Shield any warm spots with foil.
• After defrosting, let small cuts or pieces stand for 5 minutes and large cuts for 15 to 30 minutes before cooking.
• Microwave at Defrost (30%).

FOOD	MINUTES PER LB (500 G)
Meat: ground	8 to 10
chunks	4 to 8
ribs, chops	4 to 8
roasts	9 to 11
Chicken: pieces	6 to 9
whole	10 to 12
Fish: fillets	5 to 6
whole	5 to 8

GUIDE FOR COOKING POULTRY

• Defrost poultry before cooking.
• Place whole bird, breast side down, on rack in low microwaveable dish. Turn bird over halfway through cooking time.
• Arrange chicken pieces in single layer with thickest parts toward outside of dish. Rearrange pieces halfway through cooking time.
• Shield wing tips and drumstick ends with small pieces of foil.
• Cover loosely with waxed paper to prevent spattering.
• Microwave at power level suggested below for minimum time. Add more time if necessary. Let stand 5 to 10 minutes, loosely covered with foil. Test for doneness after standing time — poultry should be fork tender, juicy and meat should come away easily from bone.

POULTRY	POWER LEVEL	COOKING TIME	INTERNAL TEMP. AFTER COOKING
Turkey—whole	High for 10 min. Medium (50%) for remaining time	12 to 15 min. per lb (25 to 35 min. per kg)	180° F (85° C)
Chicken—whole	High	6 to 8 min. per lb (11 to 15 min. kg)	— —
—pieces	High	6 to 8 min. per lb (13 to 18 min. per kg)	— —

• See Poultry section for more tips and recipes.

GUIDE FOR COOKING FISH

• Remove head and tail from whole fish or shield with foil.
• Arrange fish fillets or steaks with thickest portions toward outside of dish or fold thin ends of fillets under for uniform cooking.
• Cover with lid or vented plastic wrap.
• Microwave at power level suggested below for minimum time. Add more time if necessary. Rearrange pieces halfway through cooking time.
• Fish is best if slightly undercooked and allowed to stand 5 minutes to complete cooking. Fully cooked fish will flake easily with a fork.

FISH	POWER LEVEL	COOKING TIME
Whole	High	5 to 8 min. per lb (500 g)
Fillets	High	4 to 6 min. per lb (500 g)
Salmon Steaks	Medium (50%)	6 to 8 min. per lb (500 g)

• See Fish and Seafood section for more tips and recipes.

GUIDE FOR COOKING MEAT

- *Place roast, fat side down, on microwaveable roasting rack or on rack set in shallow baking dish.*
- *Season to taste with herbs or spices. Do not salt.*
- *Cover beef or lamb with waxed paper to prevent spattering. Cover pork with lid or vented plastic wrap to ensure even cooking.*
- *Halfway through cooking, drain off excess fat or pan juices. Turn roast over and rotate dish. Shield edges or thin ends of meat, or exposed bone ends with small pieces of foil.*

- *Microwave at power level suggested below for minimum time. Check internal temperature; return to microwave oven if necessary.*
- *Let stand, tented with foil, for 10 to 20 minutes to allow internal temperature to rise and meat to "set" for ease of carving.*

MEAT	POWER LEVEL	DEGREE OF DONENESS	COOKING TIME	INTERNAL TEMP. AFTER COOKING	INTERNAL TEMP. AFTER STANDING TIME
Beef—boneless	Medium-Low (30%)	Rare	14 to 17 min. per lb (31 to 38 min. per kg)	130 °F (55 °C)	140 °F (60 °C)
	Medium-Low (30%)	Medium-Rare	16 to 18 min. per lb (36 to 39 min. per kg)	140 °F (60 °C)	150 °F (65 °C)
	Medium-Low (30%)	Medium	18 to 20 min. per lb (39 to 44 min. per kg)	150 °F (65 °C)	160 °F (70 °C)
Pork—boneless	Medium-Low (30%)	Well-Done (no pink in center)	22 min. per lb (48 min. per kg)	160 °F (70 °C)	170 °F (80 °C)
—bone in	Medium-Low (30%)	Well-Done (no pink in center)	20 min. per lb (44 min. per kg)	160 °F (70 °C)	170 °F (80 °C)
Lamb—boneless	Medium (50%)	Rare	9 to 14 min. per lb (20 to 31 min. per kg)	125 °F (52 °C)	140 °F (60 °C)
	Medium (50%)	Medium-Rare	11 to 15 min. per lb (24 to 33 min. per kg)	135 °F (57 °C)	150 °F (65 °C)
	Medium (50%)	Well-Done	13 to 16 min. per lb (24 to 33 min. per kg)	145 °F (62 °C)	160 °F (70 °C)
—bone in	Medium (50%)	Rare	8 to 12 min. per lb (18 to 27 min. per kg)	125 °F (52 °C)	140 °F (60 °C)
	Medium (50%)	Medium-Rare	10 to 14 min. per lb (22 to 30 min. per kg)	135 °F (57 °C)	150 °F (65 °C)
	Medium (50%)	Well-Done	12 to 15 min. per lb (26 to 33 min. per kg)	145 °F (62 °C)	160 °F (70 °C)

- *See Beef, Pork, Lamb and Veal Section for more tips and recipes.*

MICROWAVE REHEATING GUIDE

FOOD	POWER LEVEL	TIME	DIRECTIONS
plate of food	Medium-High (70%)	1-1/2 to 2-1/2 minutes	Cover loosely with waxed paper.
mug of tea, coffee or cider	High	1 to 2 minutes	
1 cup (250 mL) milk	High	1 to 2 minutes	Use 4-cup (1 L) measure.
1 roll, bagel or croissant	Medium-Low (30%)	20 to 30 seconds	Wrap in paper towel.
4 rolls, bagels or croissants	Medium-Low (30%)	30 to 60 seconds	Wrap in paper towel.
Casseroles: 1 serving 4 servings	Medium-High (70%) Medium-High (70%)	1-1/2 to 2 minutes 6 to 10 minutes	Cover with lid or vented plastic wrap; stir once. Allow standing time.
Frozen casseroles: 1 serving 4 servings	Medium-High (70%) Medium-High (70%)	6 to 10 minutes 12 to 15 minutes	Cover with lid or vented plastic wrap; stir once. Rotate layered casseroles once. Allow standing time.
Fruit pies: 1 slice whole pie	Medium-Low (30%) Medium-Low (30%)	1 to 1-1/2 minutes 2 to 3 minutes	Cover with paper towel.

DETERMINING YOUR MICROWAVE OVEN'S OUTPUT

If you have misplaced your owner's manual or can't find the wattage output marked on your microwave oven, here is a simple test to use:
Into a 2-cup (500 mL) microwaveable glass measure, pour 1 cup (250 mL) tap water, at room temperature. Microwave, uncovered, at High for 3 minutes. If the water boils in 3 minutes or less, your oven probably has 600 watts or more of output. If the water has not boiled in the 3 minutes, your oven probably has less than 600 watts of output.

MICROWAVE SHORTCUTS

Make your microwave pay with these easy everyday shortcuts.

• *Soften butter or cream cheese: Microwave 1/2 cup (125 mL) at Medium-Low (30%) for 20 to 40 seconds or until softened.*

• *Toast nuts and coconut: Spread 1/2 cup (125 mL) evenly on microwaveable glass pie plate. Microwave at High for 2 to 4 minutes, stirring often, just until lightly toasted.*

• *Soften ice cream: Microwave 4 cups (1 L) hard ice cream at Medium-Low (30%) for about 1 minute or until softened but not melted.*

• *Melt chocolate: Microwave 1 oz (30 g) chocolate at Medium (50%) for 2 minutes, stirring occasionally or until melted. Microwave 1/2 lb (250 g) chopped chocolate at Medium (50%) for 6 to 8 minutes, stirring occasionally.*

• *Make chocolate curls: Microwave 2 oz (60 g) chocolate at Medium (50%) for about 30 seconds or until slightly softened but not melting. Using a sharp vegetable peeler, peel off curls, rewarming chocolate square if necessary.*

• *Freshen and crisp snack foods that have lost their crunch such as potato chips, pretzels or popcorn: Place 2 cups (500 mL) on paper towel-lined plate and microwave, uncovered, at High for 30 to 60 seconds or until warm to the touch. Let cool and serve.*

• *Clarify butter: Place 1/2 cup (125 mL) butter in 2-cup (500 mL) measure. Microwave at High for 1-1/2 to 2 minutes or until boiling. Remove from microwave; skim froth from top. Let stand until separated. The clear top layer is clarified butter. Discard milk solids left at bottom.*

• *Soften squash for easy cutting: Microwave pierced whole squash at High for 2 to 3 minutes.*

• *Dissolve unflavored gelatin: Sprinkle gelatin over the liquid as specified in recipe. Let stand for 1 minute; microwave at Medium (50%) for 30 seconds to 1 minute or until gelatin has dissolved.*

• *Dry herbs: Place 1/2 cup (125 mL) fresh parsley, basil, tarragon, sage or oregano leaves between 2 sheets of paper towelling. Microwave at High for 1-1/2 to 2-1/2 minutes, stirring once, or until crumbly.*

• *Soften brown sugar: In bowl, top 1 cup (250 mL) hard brown sugar with a slice of bread or piece of apple; set on small piece of waxed paper. Cover and microwave at High for 30 to 60 seconds or until brown sugar is softened. Let stand for 5 minutes.*

• *Make croutons: Place 2 cups (500 mL) bread cubes in single layer in shallow dish. Microwave at High for 3 to 4 minutes or until crisp, stirring once.*

• *Get more juice from citrus fruit: Microwave 1 whole orange, lemon or lime at High for 30 seconds. Cut and squeeze.*

Acknowledgments and Credits

THE CONTRIBUTORS

The names of the contributing food writers are included with the recipe titles in this index for your easy reference. The recipes are organized by page number.

RECIPE TITLE	CONTRIBUTOR	PAGE
Pears with Anise	Linda Stephen	149
Chocolate Mocha Pudding	Grace Mayers	152
Rich Vanilla Pudding	Margaret Fraser	153
Pear and Cranberry Crisp	Margaret Fraser	154
Cucumber Sauce	Grace Mayers	159
Zucchini and Pepper Relish	Elizabeth Baird	162
Plum Jam	Elizabeth Baird	163
Granola	Margaret Fraser	164

The remaining recipes in this cookbook, as well as the handy charts and microwave hints, were developed in the *Canadian Living* test kitchen by test kitchen manager **Patricia Jamieson** and her staff. Special thanks to staff member **Janet Cornish** for her creativity and persistence in microwave recipe development.

MICROWAVE COOKING CONSULTANTS

Louise Dawe is the author of *Microwave Cooking Tips and Times,* a helpful, thorough reference guide. She is also the microwave consultant for Beaumark® microwave ovens.

Grace Mayers is a freelance home economist and food writer who runs her own microwave cooking school in Oshawa, Ontario.

Wendy Sanford, manager of consumer relations for Corning Canada Inc., is a home economist and contributing food writer to *Canadian Living.*

PHOTOGRAPHY CREDITS

Fred Bird: jacket front and flap; pages 17, 19, 21, 22, 25, 27, 29, 31, 35, 36, 39, 41, 42, 45, 47, 48, 51, 53, 54, 61, 66, 67, 68, 71, 72, 76, 79, 81, 83, 91, 93, 97, 103, 109, 114, 117, 118, 123, 125, 126, 129, 130, 133, 136, 139, 140, 142, 145, 147, 148, 151, 152, 155, 157, 158, 161, 165.

Skip Dean: pages 59, 64, 100, 105, 106, 110.

Nancy Shanoff: pages 88, 94.

John Stephens: pages 63, 70, 99, 121.

Stanley Wong: pages 32, 57, 85, 87, 113, 135.

Food Styling Coordinator: **Margaret Fraser**

Food Stylists: **Jennifer McLagan**
　　　　　　　 Olga Truchan

Props Coordinator: **Debby Boyden**

The publisher would like to thank the following for the use of various props for photography:

Cover: china from Villeroy and Boch, linen from Bleu Nuit; page 19: china and glassware from Villeroy and Boch; utensils from Bleu Nuit; page 22: china from Rosenthal, cutlery from Jean Couzon; page 29: china and wooden bowl from Thomas, utensils from Jean Couzon; page 36: plates and glasses from Danesco, walkman from Sony; page 42: china from Rosenthal; page 117: linen from Bleu Nuit; page 136: cookie tin, jam pot, racks and mitts from The Compleat Kitchen; page 140: china from Villeroy and Boch; page 145: china from Hutschereuther; page 157: china from Thomas.

Canadian Living would also like to thank Matsushita Electric of Canada Ltd., Toshiba of Canada Ltd. and Camco Inc. for the use of Panasonic, Toshiba and General Electric microwave ovens.

Illustrator: **Elaine Macpherson**

The microwave oven diagram on page 9 was reproduced from *The Microwave Cooking Handbook* with the permission of the International Microwave Power Institute.

Index

C

Q

Design and Art Direction:	Gordon Sibley Design Inc.
Editorial:	Hugh Brewster
	Catherine Fraccaro
Editorial Assistance:	Shirley Knight Morris
	Beverley Renahan
Production:	Susan Barrable
	Pamela Yong
Typography:	Q-Composition Inc.
Jacket Film Separation:	Colour Technologies
Color Separation, Printing and Binding:	New Interlitho S.p.A.
Canadian Living Advisory Board:	Robert A. Murray
	Judy Brandow
	Carol Ferguson
	Margaret Fraser

THE CANADIAN LIVING MICROWAVE COOKBOOK
was produced by Madison Press Books under
the direction of A.E. Cummings.